# THIS WAS
# JUST THE WAY

# THIS WAS
# JUST THE WAY

*A Memoir*

TED STAMP

TATE PUBLISHING
AND ENTERPRISES, LLC

Published by Tate Publishing & Enterprises, LLC
127 E. Trade Center Terrace | Mustang, Oklahoma 73064 USA
1.888.361.9473 | www.tatepublishing.com

Tate Publishing is committed to excellence in the publishing industry. The company reflects the philosophy established by the founders, based on Psalm 68:11,
*"The Lord gave the word and great was the company of those who published it."*

Book design copyright © 2016 by Tate Publishing, LLC. All rights reserved.
*Cover design by Samson Lim*
*Interior design by Shieldon Alcasid*

Published in the United States of America

ISBN: 978-1-68333-338-8
1. Biography & Autobiography / General
2. Biography & Autobiography / People with Disabilities
16.06.02

*For everyone who has suffered untold loss,*
*even to the point of losing hope.*

*And for my dear parents and sister, who have*
*been with me through thick and thin.*

Circumstances are like feather beds—very
comfortable to be on top of, but immensely
smothering if they get on top of you.

—Reader Harris

And we know that for those who love God all
things work together for good, for those who are
called according to his purpose.

—Romans 8:28

# PROLOGUE

# MIND OVER MATTER

FROM TIME TO time I fondly remember the solo visits I would occasionally make to Grandma Boetel's apartment. Sometimes we brought her to the house—and Grandpa, too, before he passed—either on a holiday or for one of the family birthday or anniversary parties. I remember the centerpiece of ninety bright yellow roses Mom put together for Grandpa's ninetieth, and how nervous Grandma would get as I quickly spun her wheelchair around and hoisted her backwards up the front steps. Otherwise one or both of us kids would tag along with Mom now and then when she had something to pick up or drop off over there. I wish I could say that fondness and compassion were the primary motivators of my own visits, but truth be told they were mostly the result of Mom's persistent reminders. And since I had a car to call my own—sponsored by the very one making the request—there wasn't much room for argument.

Grandpa had died at ninety, and Grandma would as well, but in the meantime—about a year—she remained in the same apartment they shared at Sunquest Village, an assisted-living facility a couple miles from our house. Hardening of the arteries and loss of circulation had resulted in the amputation of one of her legs from the knee down, and yet she still got around her small apartment fairly well in that sturdy old hospital wheelchair. But it seemed that whenever I happened to visit she had already transferred herself to the couch (or *davenport*, as she would call it), where she spent the afternoons watching soap operas or the Minnesota Twins as she crocheted the colorful *afghans* we all eventually received as birthday gifts. And of course that steel-frame chair sitting there empty was far too great a temptation to resist, and in no time flat I'd be popping wheelies every few feet, moving quickly from room to room as Grandma inevitably called out behind me, "Be careful!" This became standard procedure every visit. Greet Grandma with a kiss, make small talk, tour the apartment, have a bowl of ice cream, kiss Grandma goodbye—the only exception being, when Sarah came along, the clash we'd have over who got first crack at the chair. For the most part, that was visiting Grandma. I can't speak for Sarah, but in *my* mind I'd done my good turn for the week.

One day I brought one of my friends along. Watching me undertake my usual routine, it wasn't long before he wanted his own turn in the driver's seat. Away he went, beaming from ear to ear, into each room and right back out. And then I again, and then he, and I, and he, until eventually, probably very nonchalantly, one of us happened to open the front door, which gave way to a long, vacant hallway. Instantly the same idea seemed to dawn upon us both, and without a word the pilot, turned passenger, lifted his feet as copilot suddenly broke into a sprint behind him, pushing Grandma's chair far beyond the limits of its design. The combined chorus of quaking wheels and shrieks of laughter was stifled only by a mutual effort to avoid both walls and pedestrians. And of course back and forth pilot and copilot took their joyful turns, until, as always, novelty inevitably turned drudgery.

It's a sweet memory that reminds me of the ironic naivety of youth. How this mindset often proves to be the mother of spontaneous, creative, memorable ideas and experiences, yet just as often while remaining totally oblivious to the obvious. What I'm getting at is that I can remember thinking during one of those visits—while wheeling around in that tired chair and seeing helpless Grandma there on the couch—of the strangeness of old age and the limitations implicit in her need of the chair. It seemed utterly inconceivable to me that such restriction and vulnerability could ever, or would ever, have any effect on me. It simply seemed to me a thing which needed to be renounced, a ripe occasion for mind and will to triumph over matter. Need I say more?

# IT SO HAPPENED

DAD WAS JUST nineteen when he made up his mind to leave the family farm and enlist in the air force. He'd had enough of chores and farm work and found his ticket out. Four years later, he returned to his roots, or thereabouts, a little older and wiser. First to Fargo, where he went to auto body school courtesy of the G.I. Bill, then to Huron, where his uncle had offered him a job at the Huron Body Shop. He volunteered as a firefighter and even lived at the fire hall for a time, filling in as an ambulance driver as needed. Mom also left the farm at eighteen, though she for South Dakota State University. A little more than four years later, she was living in Sioux Falls and teaching physical education at Patrick Henry Junior High and Lincoln High School. They both played league softball in their respective towns and first crossed paths at a tournament somewhere or other. They don't say much about the rest. It wasn't a shotgun wedding, I know that much. "It was a long time ago," they say.

I was a miracle—an answer to prayer, in fact—having arrived after six discouraging years of unsuccessful trying, including a miscarriage. They had almost given up and adopted. By the time I finally came along, the bittersweet fruit of eighteen hours of labor, Dad was forty and Mom thirty-four. Sarah followed two years later. We lived on Frank Street in the house that Grandpa and Grandma Boetel moved into after we moved out, when I turned three. From there we moved into the house I would call home for the next fifteen years, where my parents still live.

They had married before all that, though, and the G.I. Bill also got them a reduced interest loan on that first house. Aside from that, neither had any debt, though neither had much in the way of assets, either, unless you count us kids. Mom had been working for a friend as a florist, though she stayed home with us kids from when we were born until we started grade school. By then Dad had moved on to another job at the Ford dealership and then eventually opened his own body shop. Several years later, Mom started her own flower shop as well. We never moved, not even within Huron, and they never divorced. I don't even remember them ever raising their voices at one another. There is, however, an old story that gets brought up every now and then (usually with the relatives around) about when Dad tried to take Mom antelope hunting in those early years before kids. "That was as close as I ever came to leaving," Mom half-jokes. Their friends were their age and were neither party people nor night owls. They were adults with careers and children of their own, and when they got together they'd sit out on the patio having a few beers as they talked and told stories and laughed. And it was all so civil and easygoing, as if no one had a care in the world.

I never wondered why Mom and Dad so spoiled us, though they don't think they did, even to this day. I guess I probably figured that's what parents were supposed to do. It's interesting to think about what motivates people to act one way rather than another, especially when it's people who happened to have had an enormous influence on your life. So much is determined by what we grew up either taking or not taking for granted.

"We were poor," I've heard them both say so many times about the way they grew up. Never complaining, just saying. "Not as poor as some, though," they are always careful to add. "We never once went hungry."

Think rural South Dakota farmsteads in the Dirty Thirties and early forties. Before 401(k)s and Social Security. Think year-round outhouses (Sears catalogs or newspaper to clean up). Little or no electricity. Wood-burning stoves. Artesian well water carried in by the bucketful from outside. Hand-scrubbed laundry. Fresh-baked bread and chickens butchered daily.

"We didn't know any different," is what Dad says when you ask him things like why they regularly ate something called *mush* and drank water that was brown. The year his family secured a loan to build a house, he and one or two siblings had to sleep out in a loft in the garage for many months, even winter months. Their mother would send them out into the dark with bricks she'd warmed in the stove, which were wrapped up in pillowcases they'd warm their feet on until they fell asleep. Even until they were almost ten, he and his three siblings bathed in the same washbasin of water once a week, one after the other, oldest to youngest, which meant Dad went last. Auntie Marge, one of the oldest (she's a twin) and the only girl, always got to go first. Years later she broke the news—with a cute but mischievous giggle, I should add—that she sometimes peed in there.

Their parents never said to them, "I love you," as far as they remember, but they say they were loved no less. It was a different generation, different times. It brings to mind the time Dad told me how his dad had lent him money to start his body shop. When the day arrived that he happily handed his dad the check to pay him back, he was surprised to hear him respond, "Where's the interest?" And whereas one person so treated might very naturally turn around and make such a policy their own, we grew up taking for granted the love of a father and mother who, though they knew so little in the way of advantages, lavished upon us every privilege they could. And if there were a banner that waved over our upbringing, it might've read: "Good measure, pressed down, shaken together, running over, continually poured into our laps."

# THE KIND OF THINGS
# YOU WERE TAUGHT

In our household, every night before bed you'd get a visit from Mom and Dad, one shortly after the other, and a kiss on the forehead, and a "Sleep well, honey. I love you"— every night, without fail. By high school you didn't get the personal room visit, but when you weren't coming in late and they saw you before they turned in, you always at least heard the words, which were always more than just words.

When you were very young—exactly how young isn't clear—Mom sat on the bed with you and taught you other words—something like a poem—to say to One you couldn't see or hear. It surprises you, recalling them, how they've stayed with you for so long, through thick and thin, though you no longer say them that way. They have become a part of you, the way a scar becomes part of your face. How intently you must have listened. From as far back as you can remember, every night alone in bed, you'd repeat the gentle words, usually slowly enough to think about the meaning of each line. How many times your cheeks were wet with tears. There was something right about the words, something true, though you couldn't put your finger on what it was. They grounded you. Gave you a feeling of rest deep within. You'd quietly mouth them to yourself when staying the night at the houses of friends or out in a tent in the back yard or in a hotel room in another town. Sometimes you'd even crawl out of bed and get on your knees, convicted by their simple purity. Even throughout high school, when you were too cool to give Dad a hug or Mom a kiss in front of friends, once the lights went out you found yourself unconsciously with folded hands.

> *Now the light has gone away,*
> *Father, listen while I pray,*
> *Asking You to watch and keep*
> *And to send me quiet sleep.*
> *Jesus, Tender Shepherd, hear me,*
> *Bless your little lamb tonight.*
> *Through the darkness be Thou near me,*
> *Keep me safe 'til morning light.*
> *May my sins be all forgiven,*
> *Bless the friends I love so well,*
> *Take us all to heaven at last,*
> *Happy there with You to dwell.*
> *Amen.*

It makes you wonder where these words came from, how old they are, and how and when Mom had them taught to her. It makes you wonder how and why you do the things you do and believe what you believe. There were also words to say before each meal—different ones, but again the same ones every time so that you knew them like your name. Though these were said in unison so quickly it was hard to let their meaning fill your mind. And afterwards the table-talk commenced so quickly that if you wanted something out of them you'd have to think them through some other time.

This was the hand you just so happened to be dealt. A world shot through at every point with better than you deserve, where you were frequently hearing things like: *If you don't have anything nice to say, don't say anything at all*, or *Treat others the way you'd want them to treat you*, or *Share and share alike*, or C*ount your blessings*. Things that made plain sense, with which you could hardly argue. One moment you'd be demonstrating in word or deed your shortsighted and selfish meanness or stupidity, and one of these sayings would cut you off and lodge itself into your memory banks for life. You might have whined and fussed, arguing your side, but in the end their logic got the better of you, and before long you'd find yourself saying the same things.

And this while so many other kids you knew were learning different things, at the very least a much more colorful vocabulary, or that this life is all there is, and then you take a dirt nap and all you are is worm food. Just imagine how much differently you might look at worms and everything else.

# NINJA RUNS

WHEN I WAS small they struck our house—nameless, faceless phantoms. Probably the older kids down the block, I thought, who chased us on our bikes one time. It was Mom's flower garden on the south, which was tilled up for the season, just outside their bedroom window, where I had left my many matchbox cars—most of which were gone or smashed to bits. I even found some in the gutters halfway down the street. I cried and wondered why. Did they not understand that they were mine?

It doesn't matter whose they are. I came to understand that plain enough. A little later—several years—when I somehow found it fun with friends—a group of three or five or more—to be out late and wandering in the dark, unsupervised. To walk the alleys and the streets in search of nothing in particular. It was something to do and appealed to your adventurous side. It wasn't every month or even every six months, only as often as someone might suggest and lead the way.

You put on your darkest shirts and pants and lightest shoes. You looked for things to grab along the way—lawn ornaments or decorations, or even just long sticks to swing around. It's amazing what you find in people's yards. Sometimes it was a gnome or silly toy we took, or even something as big as a kiddie pool or birdbath. Imagine dragging a birdbath down the street and laughing hysterically while at the same time trying to keep your voice down. Sometimes you had to climb beneath or overtop a fence. Sometimes a garbage can got tipped or banged on like a dinner bell, and you had to run for it with everything in you for a couple blocks, cutting across lawns and leaping over random obstacles, breathless and full of adrenaline. Maybe that was part of the draw. The later it got, the clearer you could hear your footsteps clomping down the street. The barking dogs got louder too. The jangling of their chains made you nervous, especially the bigger dogs. Here and there a floodlight or a set of headlights flashed, and you'd break into a sprint and then slow down again. False alarm. But eventually your legs got tired or the novelty wore off, and you all went your separate ways.

When we used a car, it only increased our efficiency and ability to stow and go. On one occasion it was a newspaper machine, taking the whole stack for the quarter we put in. We were after coupons for sub sandwiches, plenty for each of us, and that seemed like a foolproof plan. What did we do with the rest of the papers? Out the window as we gutted them, assembly-line style, driving down a lonesome country road. Another time it was pop machines. Someone had a key, and so we drove around one night on the lookout for that particular brand, and when we stopped someone would run up and give it a quick try, as the other three sat tight, looking every which way nervously.

Now and then you might have seen our names or pictures in the paper—sometimes for good grades or athletic or other recognitions—and you never would have guessed that it was us. We were some of the "good kids."

And all the while, with things like this and more, you always heard the voice that never lets you off the hook. The one that doesn't take sides and always tells it like it is—the one that says, at the very least, "You know better than this."

# OF GOD AND CONSCIENCE

I COULDN'T SAY whether or not I have an overly sensitive conscience. How would you go about determining that? It's not like comparing yourself with others helps you much. Conscience has to do with what we know, and how we think and act in accord with that knowledge. So while it seems to function the same way within us all—which I have heard referred to as "the impartial spectator"—it also functions uniquely in us all according to our various capacities and personalities.

This brings to mind a memorable experience from my childhood, for whatever it's worth. My sister and I were down the street at the house of one of our neighbors for the evening. The girl was in my class and the boy in my sister's, and I was friends with the younger and Sarah the older. Our parents and theirs had gone out for the evening and decided to leave us without a babysitter, which I have a feeling we managed to convince them would be okay (we older ones might have been ten or eleven at the time). At one point we, for some reason, wanted to leave their house and go to ours instead, which we did, though we felt we needed a good reason to justify this, so as to avoid trouble. So when the parents came home, we said something to the effect that a strange man was pounding on the front door and wouldn't go away, and we were terrified, so we decided to slip out the back door and run for it down to our house. We relayed the story with plenty of dramatic gestures and breathless suspense, and as you might imagine they were quite taken aback by it. It probably didn't do much for our case of ever staying home alone again, but at least they seemed to buy it. But as I lay in my bed that night, I found myself unable to sleep. And when I could take no more, I tiptoed into Mom and Dad's room and spilled the beans about our little ruse.

Around our house, weekly Sunday school and church attendance were almost never optional for us kids, and only the most convincing feigned sickness could rarely rescue us from that regime. The immortal words of Grandma Boetel were regularly invoked, that if you could stay up late on Saturday evening, you could get up for church on Sunday morning.

Probably the closest I ever felt to God growing up was in the seventh and eighth grade. It was during these tender years that my church classmates and I were passing through the last two years of "confirmation" classes that would make us eligible for official church membership. This rite of passage took place every Wednesday after school for about two hours and was more rigorous than any of our public school classes. In addition to learning about sixteenth century reformer, Martin Luther, we were taught from his Small Catechism, which doesn't seem so small when you fine-tooth-comb it the way we did. We memorized the Lord's Prayer, the Ten Commandments, the Nicene Creed, the Apostle's Creed, and each of their responsive explanations—all of which were, with the exception of the Ten Commandments, routinely recited in church liturgy. We memorized the names, genres, and overall structure of the sixty-six books of the Bible, as well as heaping helpings of its verses. We memorized pages and pages of our own handwritten notes concerning specific church teachings and other details. Lengthy written tests followed each section, including midterms and finals, and eventually, as the capstone, public confession of various portions before the church body.

If you passed, it formally reaffirmed the "faith" that had been allegedly created in you during your baptism as an infant. Gaining membership meant the beginning of responsibility in the church, a commitment not just to maintain regular church attendance but also to give financially and be involved in other church affairs. It meant starting to consider the things of God in a more mature light than you had or could as a child. But above all, membership meant access to the communion table, the bread and the wine of the forgiveness of sins.

But there were always questions percolating just below the surface. It can be unsettling to think through what you believe and why you believe it, especially at that age. There's always the chance you might discover something you didn't expect, maybe something more than you wanted to know, and then you'd be left to wrestle with the implications. Not that you ever thought things through that much back then. After all, what fun was memorizing a bunch of jargon you couldn't see the point in when you could be out skateboarding or shooting hoops or lighting something on fire? And so most of the time you put those thoughts off for later, maybe someday when you were older and could appreciate them like all the adults seemed to. They took these things for granted, and it felt awkward to ask questions, as if they might answer you that those things ought to be self-evident. But then they were always so supportive, and there was the promise of reward once it was all over with, and the fact that it would make them happy. And you wanted that.

Meanwhile, I took pride and comfort in the golden cross I sometimes wore around my neck through most of high school, even outside my shirt. I couldn't deny that deep down there seemed to be something noble about believing in God, something that set you apart from others. It made plain sense when, on warm summer nights, lying on your back in the lawn, you'd gaze deeply into the immense blackness of a star-filled night, full of searching questions. It gave you a sense of where you came from and where you were going. And then there was the fact that from a young age I was haunted by the fear of death, picturing now and then as I lay in bed at night the cemetery not far from our house, and myself buried there one day, the howling wind blowing right over my tombstone without flinching and leaving me and the memory of my life to be forgotten forever. All I could do back then was scurry into Mom and Dad's room and dive beneath the covers, where all seemed safe and sound. Death seemed so terribly cruel and final, and the idea of a mysterious God somewhere far above the heavens always helped relieve a heavy heart.

And so in the end I did my duty and jumped through all the necessary hoops.

A few buddies and I after graduation, 1993

Leaving for Boys' State, 1992

# YOUR AVERAGE NICE GUY

I'M SORTING THROUGH old pictures in the hope of coming into contact with who I was those last couple years of high school. A couple in particular stand out. There's the homecoming royalty one, with all of us so polished in our ties and button-up shirts and dresses, smiling pretty for the camera, the "king" and "queen" in the middle— such a strange little tradition. And then the one with five of my buddies and I in our graduation garb just after the ceremony, bright-eyed and arm in arm, on top of the world. Each one is definitely worth at least a thousand words, but none of them gets me too much closer to understanding the mindset I only vaguely remember.

It's funny that nothing in me whatsoever cares to go back. It seems like another life altogether, which it really was. As much as the pictures reveal, they don't tell the whole story. It makes me wonder if the "thousand words" that a picture is worth refers to what is obvious, or also to the things you have to rely on memory to bring back. You'd never know, for example, looking at the graduation one, that I'd had three beers an hour or so before the ceremony, just to keep my nerves in check. And it's little details like that make you ask yourself, *Just who was I, anyway? What did any of us really know about anything?* We were all so immersed in ourselves and immersed in the moment.

I'm wondering what, in particular, made me tick, though maybe it's an exercise in futility. I had to ask myself, *What if the way you remember yourself isn't the way others remember you?* I wonder what people would say. I think they would probably say that I was a nice guy. I kind of had a reputation for that. Not that I always was (look no further than my sister and her friends for your first character witnesses). I imagine there are several people who still remember me as something of a jerk, and I truly was sometimes. Most of the time, though, I was pretty nice to everyone and got along with people fairly far removed from my social clique. So that was part of what made me who I was.

There's a lot that could be said about what shapes us into the people we become. There are countless influences to consider. Being Mister Nice Guy was not something I woke up in the morning trying to be, and if that was really how I was perceived, I don't think it was before I turned sixteen. It's such a funny transformation we go through as children and teenagers, so many phases and modes of personality we take on. By my senior year I was very friendly, polite, and respectful, for the most part, respected by most of my teachers and classmates, as well as by the parents of my friends. But like the pictures, so much of it was surface deep. There was one persona for dealing with adults and another for hanging with friends. Not that it was an entirely two-faced existence without consistency, but it certainly wasn't authentic. It's hard to put it in a nutshell.

The main thing I notice about the pictures is how young we all look, even as seniors. I can remember as a freshman and even a sophomore looking up to the seniors as being so grown-up and possessing a sort of godlike status. We felt like such inconsequential peons in comparison, though maybe I should speak for myself. That's what made peer pressure seem so daunting and hard to resist sometimes. It's really amazing the kind of power that unspoken status wielded without anyone ever saying a word about it. But when we got to be those seniors, it didn't feel that way, nor do I remember even being conscious of it much. But probably a lot of what I said and did affected those around me more than I would care to know. Looking at these pictures, though, I keep thinking, *We were all just kids.*

# JUNE 29, 1993

# A NEW JOB PROSPECT

My first official job was cross-pollinating corn for Pioneer Seed when I was fourteen. Remember fourteen? Those were the days, when you were daily discovering new ways to stand on your own two feet. The most exciting way was by getting your driver's license. For better and worse that little chunk of plastic unlocked the door to so many new possibilities, the privilege of going almost anywhere you wished at the drop of a hat—sometimes even where you didn't so much wish. Even just holding onto the keys was a thrill. You felt all grown up. Dad had even bought me a little pale-yellow beater to call my own, a '77 Chevette with velveteen seats, AM radio, and no air conditioning. It wasn't much to look at, inside or out, but it was all mine, and that's all that mattered then. I'm not sure what exactly prompted me to take the job. Dad had suggested it, probably given all his farmer connections out in Uncle Lyle's neck of the country. And he wasn't without good reason, since most summer days he came home from a hard day's work to his string bean son sprawled out in front of a blaring television, often murmuring of how bored he was.

In any case, it wasn't as though the job was my first brush with hard work, if that's what it was, though I'm not so sure. One thing was sure, when you had parents who were both raised on semi-subsistence farms in the wake of the Great Depression, you were not about to get away with lying around for hours on end. Not without being told to get up and wash or dry dishes, rake or mow the lawn, scoop snow, sweep the garage, stack wood, and all the rest. And Mom was so gracious. She'd come home from a full day of work just in time to hear us ask what's for supper—"Dry bread and water," she loved to say with a smirk—which she promptly got to work on. Usually Dad had to give us the head signal to give her a hand with whatever she was in the process of doing, probably thinking (rightly) that if she didn't do it, it wouldn't get done. He'd also remind us now and then (usually around Mother's Day) to take the initiative and do some of these things before she got home.

Every now and then there was even the chance to taste the chores at Uncle Lyle's—lugging around numerous five-gallon buckets full of feed and water, or taking up pitchfork and shovel to clean out a putrefied hog pen; fixing fence, picking rock, tossing bales, butchering chickens. All you got was a taste every now and then, and you were more than a little thankful for that. But you still got a taste, and years later you'd thank God for that. And for this and the little we did around the house, whining all the while, we were given all the cash a kid could need. I remember so often telling them, "No, no, I have enough," which my buddies could hardly believe. All we had to do was keep our grades up and stay out of trouble. So really there wasn't much reason to have a job except more spending money.

But for whatever reason I got the job, and every morning about half past seven I'd crawl, sleepy-eyed, into that old hatchback and drive the nine or so miles out to the crowded corn fields just beyond Uncle Lyle's. Windows down, music blasting, gas pedal pinned to the floor most of the way, that faithful little beast shivered and whined all the way down that lonely stretch of well-worn blacktop. It's a miracle I ever made it out there and back in one piece. I was just one among a scrubby throng of kids my age or a little older who had converged from a number of neighboring small towns (*really* small towns). Our task was to walk down row after eternal row of ripening corn and staple paper bags over the tassels of each stalk, which collected the pollen. Then sometime later we tromped back down those same clumpy rows and removed the bags, this time re-stapling them over the silky-smooth ears of each stalk. Even more unrelenting than this monotony were the multitudes of mosquitoes and steadily increasing heat and humidity. Not sure what to expect from a first job, I bit my lip and swatted my arms and legs day after day, setting my hopes on the promised group trip to Valley Fair at the end of the summer, which did pretty well soak up your sorrows once you got there. I don't recall if I came back for a second summer of it, but if I did, that Valley Fair trip would've been the only reason.

Sometime after my freshman year of high school, probably during supper one evening, another job prospect was brought up. It was another summer job apparently held by a number of high school students and returning college students during their summer break, doing general maintenance duties with the Huron Parks and Recreation Department. About anything seemed better than those hot, buggy cornfields. So I applied, and whether or not it made a difference in my favor that one of the higher-ups at Parks and Rec was an old softball friend and teammate of my Mom's from decades before, the summer following my sophomore year I had a new job.

# MY PARTICULAR ASSIGNMENT

THERE WERE ALWAYS a few mornings each summer when I'd bike to work. It was a cheaper model mountain bike with a heavy frame and hard-to-shift gears, which I had bought with some of my own hard-earned money. Even as tired as I usually was, I remember cheering myself on as I pondered how in shape I'd be by basketball season and how much gas I'd save. From our house it was a little less than a mile, and by the time I arrived I was not only quickened by the cool air but full of resolve that I'd found a new habit. On my way home for lunch, the slight decline of 18th Street for several blocks pushed me to pedal 'til my thighs burned as I tried my best to outpace traffic. I'd imagine a kind of awe sweeping over passing drivers as they noted my prowess and purposeful face. But after lunch I'd sink into the couch downstairs and kick my feet up, and by the time five to one rolled around I was full of reasons why taking my car back to work seemed the more sensible option. After all, it might rain.

My particular assignment was to be part of the five-man crew responsible for taking care of the Washington School Little League Complex, which included six baseball diamonds and the property that encompassed them. It was a large square lot in the midst of an easygoing, middle-to-upper-middle-class neighborhood, with Washington School, on the northeast corner, being the primary activity center most of the year. And while in the summer the five of us had the complex pretty much to ourselves most days, nearly every evening the grounds were buzzing with boys on bikes, bats on their shoulders and gloves on their handlebars. On game nights the flurry only intensified, when the parents swarmed to see their sons (and rarely daughters) suited up in business-sponsored jerseys—bright greens and yellows, blues and reds—their cheers and jeers being heard for several blocks. It was for these we were tasked with making the grounds look their best.

During my two-plus years there it was essentially the same five of us working together, aside from a difference in supervisors from my first year to the years after that. We were all different ages and in different graduating classes, the oldest being Dan, our supervisor, who was a premed student at the University of South Dakota, where I was soon headed, and where Chris also went, having just finished his freshman year. Tom had just finished as a sophomore at South Dakota State, and Mike (a.k.a. Rudy) was a year younger than I. So you could say there was a certain pecking order among us. But at the same time we all shared a number of interests, more than anything a love of sports and the popular culture, so it didn't take long to break through the usual, initial standoffishness. Soon enough we were slugging each other and calling one another *rookie*, joking about someday being Park and Rec *lifers* like some of the old guys on the downtown crew. And as drastically different as some of our personalities were, there was a kinship among us most days that made our daily loads seem even lighter. Most days.

If memory serves, the first time I set foot on the complex it was just Tom and I, and I can still barely make out an image or two from that encounter. It was mid-afternoon in May, I think, within the last two weeks of school getting out. I clearly remember hearing the events of some track-related activity being announced at Tiger Stadium, a few blocks away. There was probably a little awkwardness between us since we'd never met—having gone to different high schools—but whenever you have a task to share it makes connecting that much easier. And somehow we did, though it was a little surprising that we ended up hanging out as much as we did during my last two years of school, though mostly in the summer. But we liked some of the same music, played league softball, and lifted weights together, and also shared a keen interest in the gals. Among the five of us out there, our friendship was the closest.

Aside from having to bear the heat and humidity most days and get a little dirty, Parks and Rec was a dream job for guys our age. For one thing, it only lasted through the summer, and if you managed to show up and "keep your nose clean" (as Dad would say), you were pretty likely to be hired back the following summer. The workload was fairly modest and provided a steady forty-hour week, not to mention the bonus of working outside—with far fewer mosquitoes than in the corn fields—often shirtless and in shorts, which also meant an unbeatable suntan. There were also periodic opportunities for gaining weekend overtime when girls' softball tournaments came to town, though in this respect the pay was only half the incentive, as it was hardly sensible to pass up the chance to spend two full days blissfully outnumbered by girls your age.

Every job has its mix of pros and cons, but for the likes of us a guy could hardly complain.

# MY LAST DAY

ON WHAT TURNED out to be my last day of work, I happened to drive rather than bike. And whenever any of us drove, which was most days—especially when it was raining—we'd sit there in our cars along McDonald Drive with our heads leaned back against our seats, half-conscious, listening to our stereos as we waited out the last few minutes before eight.

Whether I was feeling especially lazy that morning and watched the others get out first and walk ahead of me to the big brown shed where we started each day, or they had all arrived—maybe some on bike—before I had and were already inside, it seems that it was in solitude that I casually walked that hundred-yard jaunt. Looking down, I can almost still see the canvas toes of my filthy work loafers getting wetter with each step as I made my way across that familiar tract of dew-covered grass, kicking each foot forward lightly to flick the moisture into the air. About twenty-five feet to my right was the first-base-line fence of Kuhnart Field, where the oldest teams, the Colt league, played. It was the only diamond with grass on the infield and a warning track along the back fence, like the Legion field uptown. We always felt proudest getting this one ready because it looked the best of any on the complex, like our own little version of the Big Leagues. Behind the home-plate fence stood an elevated announcer's booth, and behind that a long, mesh batting cage, and just behind that, coming up on my left, the small brickwork concession stand which housed the bathrooms and water fountain. Forbes Field, on the opposite side, hosted the Minor leaguers and sometimes even the five of us when we'd take an occasional break for a homerun derby. Back on my right, behind the batting cage, sat the shed where the guys would be waiting for me, and next to that Ambrosius, a Major-league field. A hundred-plus feet in front of me, on the left, lay the only Pony-league field, Sportsman, where as an eighth grader I shocked everyone—including myself—by hitting a home run off Pat Timm. Behind this lay the Washington School playground, and a ways to the right of that the remaining major and minor-league fields, the Met and Polo.

These were the grounds we daily traversed and groomed, sometimes gladly and other times dragging our feet. For some of us they were to some degree sacred, each field ripe with memories of yesterdays—when we were those boys on bikes, busy about our boyhood dreams.

As usual, I would have hung a right after the batting cage and walked the last thirty-odd steps to the shed. Would have seen and heard the guys sprawled out in their lawn chairs or on the ragamuffin couch we scored at the junkyard the previous summer—their pasty faces and grubby shoes, and shorts and shirts and sweats. Their murmurs of the latest scores, or movie plots, or jokes about each other's girlfriends. With maybe one exception their caps bore the logos of sports teams and the faded residue of agri-lime or base-line chalk—and if it wasn't their cap that got it at one time or other, they might have got a handful shoveled into their shoes or tossed down the back of their shorts. But that would come later, when the time was right. Before all that, we would divvy up the morning chores, a routine more regular than the rain. And who would gain the all-important first and second choice of job lay vested in the hands of but one arbiter: Rock, Paper, Scissors.

Aside from the rare opportunity to paint dugouts or other buildings, or to leave the grounds with someone to pick up supplies or dump off a tailgate-load of something or other, the chores were mostly the same every day. The next best choice in the morning was raking in batter's boxes, which after each evening's games had been shredded into sand traps by the cleats of energetic boys digging themselves in to bat. This meant you got a partner, which always made things more interesting. Together you drove a three-wheeled buggy called the Cushman from field to field and raked into the ruts on either side of home plate a mixture of clay, water, and agri-lime. Then, with footsteps squeezed closely together, you "tamped" them down until they were smooth and firm enough to please you both.

Picking up garbage was next best, since there really wasn't that much of it. Sometimes you even scored half a bag of sunflower seeds or mosquito repellent some kid left behind the previous evening. The downside was that you worked alone and had to walk the entire grounds, bending over frequently, including inside dugouts and under bleachers. If there were games the previous night, you got a partner and use of the truck to drive from field to field, collecting the heavy silver trash barrels that you then emptied into the dumpster. The downside of this was that from that point forward your skin and clothes took on a whole other kind of stink. After that came weeding, mowing, and, if necessary, siphoning infields. Bathroom duty was probably the most unpopular because you were on your own dragging a roll of garden hose in one hand and a five-gallon bucketful of cleaning supplies in the other as you took to giving those brick walls and steel stalls a most unholy frothing spray down, floor to ceiling.

We also coached T-ball two afternoons a week, which gave us the chance to be the heroes of all these kids for a few hours. I think it was Chris who liked to say that you could always tell which kids were on my team: the ones climbing all over the dugouts like wild animals. Once they cleared out, only two hours remained to prep the fields for the coming evening's games. The short end of the straw this time around meant you and your partner were stuck with dragging around the complex the six or seven heavy rolls of fire hoses for spraying down the infields, in order to keep the agri-lime dust off the neighboring houses, once the infield dragger got started. The bonus of this messy job was unleashing your frustrations with it on your unwitting coworkers if they came into range, which on the hottest days most did voluntarily. The infield dragger was the prize task of the afternoon, which simply involved driving our other three-wheeler, the Triplex, in slow, concentric circles from the pitching mound of each infield outward. The follow-up to this was the equally coveted two-man task of laying down baselines and batter's boxes on the newly smoothed-over infields, another science in itself that included a squeaky two-wheeled chalker and a dirty spool of string. Otherwise you were stuck weeding or mowing, and by that time usually under blistering sunshine and peak humidity. Although not so much that summer because of all the rain, which of course was music to our grubby little ears.

Most of us were not exactly poster boys for hard work, but what could you expect when most of us were city slickers. Overall, though, we kept those grounds looking pretty darn nice, if we didn't say so ourselves. It was actually amazing sometimes how much pride we took in some of the work. Not so much in cleaning the bathrooms or picking up garbage, but when it came to dragging infields or firming up batter's boxes or laying down meticulously straight baselines, then something mysterious took over. Though some of the mystery is dispelled when you remember how a job well done not only secured for you legitimate ground for boasting, but it also safeguarded you and your handiwork from the others' mockery.

At any rate, I don't recall whether I won or lost that morning at Rock, Paper, Scissors, or whether I worked alone or otherwise, or if it was bathrooms or garbage or siphoning that I did first. After the grumbles of the losers subsided, we likely went our separate directions as usual. But the fits of rain wouldn't let up, so all we could do was sit in the shed and wait. And when it seemed evident that it wasn't likely to stop, we left for break a little earlier than normal, heading downtown to our favorite spot, The Donut Shoppe.

# TODAY WAS A GOOD DAY

I'D BEEN LISTENING to it a lot in recent weeks, a new favorite with a catchy chorus: "Today Was a Good Day." I'm sure I'd had it on in the car that morning, since it was on my lips as I first made my way toward the shed. It's one of those memories whose survival strikes me as strangely improbable, though thinking this reminds me that the survival of *any* memory is a miracle. For whatever reason, it survived, and the Internet brought back its opening lines:

> *Just wakin' up in the morning, gotta thank God.*
> *I don't know, but today seems kinda odd.*

It was a Tuesday morning, but if there was something odd about it I must have missed it. It was dreary and rainy, not unlike most days so far that June. Most, if not all, of the infields and some parts of the outfields lay under shallow but sizable pools of standing water, and one of our new daily routines was to relocate these game-impeding ponds. It's actually one of the clearest memories I have of that summer: taking turns manually pumping bucket after five-gallon bucketful and passing them assembly-line style from infield to outfield, over and over and over again. At first glance these little lakes didn't look very significant, shallow as they seemed, and it wasn't until you got to pumping that wooden handle up and down within the aluminum shaft of the siphon a hundred times and more—your feet underwater at the base, holding it steady—or waddling another heavy bucketful one-handed to the outfield, that you truly began to appreciate what you were up against. And when one pond disappeared, it was on to the next, and when one infield was dry—relatively speaking—there was the next field. And then it would rain again. As with some of our other routines, this tedium sooner or later got the best of us in predictable ways, and before long someone got a bucketful poured over his shoes, or his cap tossed in for a swim. I don't remember if it felt like a good day or not. I imagine it felt like just another work day.

But any time you're looking through the rearview mirror this way, beware of hindsight on the prowl—given all you know now that you didn't know then. Not just the "could've-would've-should've" thoughts, but more the subtle tendency—or maybe the temptation—to speculate. To wonder, for example, what you might've thought as you sang that song. Was there something in the air or in your bones that felt peculiar? That gave away what was on the way? But what might seem from here like irony was just a song and chorus there and then. I know full well there's no going back, that the future rushing at us now is now—an instant later—history, and the only way to relive it is in your head. And every time you try you run the risk of adding or taking away from what was actually the way a thing took place.

So I was singing as I walked and there's no telling what was on my mind. It was early and the night before may well have been a late one. So they were likely groggy waking thoughts, whatever they were. Perhaps of how the summer had just begun and who could say what yet it had in store. Some reckless nights already since we'd donned our caps and gowns and put that beast of public school to rest for good. Or maybe of the girl I'd been together with a year, with whom I was as happy as naive. Or even thoughts of my third year at the fields, more money in my pockets for the fall. Probably more than all the fall was often on my mind—like a golden sunset, beckoning me, each day a little closer, rain or shine. That whole new world three hours' drive between, a smaller town with a different name, full of strangers and another kind of school. Another life with different rules, the bulk of which were yours to legislate. And your heart could hardly stand to wait. But you had no choice. You could only wake and work and stay out late—one day at a time, like everybody else, awaiting your appointed date.

With some of my Tee-ball kids, 1992 or 1993

# ALL TOO TYPICAL

I DON'T KNOW how the majority of my classmates viewed this transition in their lives. On the one hand, after multiple years of what often felt like a prison sentence, we were all showing the usual symptoms of senioritis. We birds of the same nest, poised to embark on our maiden flight, feeling a confluence of both hopeful expectation and pressure. A fair number had lofty aims, heading off with ROTC scholarships or to Ivy League schools, several of them very good friends of mine. They were taking the next four years extremely seriously, as they had always taken school. The kind of folks who spent long hours studying for their ACTs and SATs. I might've been hungover the morning I took my ACT, and in the end scored a whopping twenty-one—dead average—and probably fitting for one who had brought home mostly Bs over the years. It wasn't that I didn't think it was a crucial season in a person's life. There was always in the back of my mind the resounding mantra we had been hearing from our teachers for years, the host of ominous warnings that college was no mere day at the beach—the sign under the clock in Mrs. Buddenhagen's room said it all: *Ya Snooze, Ya Lose.* I anticipated what lay ahead as much as anyone, but like many of my classmates, with divided loyalties.

As much as my career interests had shifted over those last two years—from dentistry to meteorology to politics and government—I did know very well what I was *not* cut out to be. Neither a doctor nor lawyer nor architect nor engineer, nor even a "dumb body-man," as my Dad would put it. In fact, Dad had offered that I could take over his shop when the time was right, and Mom had said the same of hers as well. But neither appealed to me. I didn't know what I wanted, just something respectable that would allow me to live a good deal better off than we were without eight years of school or too much hard work. Something where you put the least in and got the most out. Like the lottery.

The snag was that Dad and Mom were footing the bill. It sounds terrible putting it that way now, but that's more or less how I thought of it then—a positive thing, for sure, but with strings attached. They'd been saving for us kids from before we were born and wouldn't expect even a penny in return down the road. And that was an amazing thing. They weren't holding it over us or anything, demanding that we pursue a particular course or wagging their fingers that we better not squander their hard-earned investment. Nothing remotely of the sort. Just another free gift of grace from the same ones who had been supplying so many others. But that meant that you couldn't just mess around down there. Not without a guilty conscience, anyway. That was the rub. Not that you had to use their money, but who in their right teenage mind could refuse? Which meant you'd have to commit to work hard when the time came, which conjured up unsettling words like *initiative* and *discipline* and the like.

So that last year I found myself gunning for good grades and honed habits like never before. Many times that meant turning down buddies who wanted to steal me away on a school night or Saturday afternoon, to the point that I began hearing that I needed to chill out and enjoy my senior year. It helped that for the first time ever I wasn't involved in any sports, not even basketball. By spring I'd been accepted at USD and arranged with a good friend to be roommates. I made the campus visit for preregistration of classes and all the standard orientation. Declared a major in Political Science. Toured the various buildings and dorm rooms. Pictured how the bunks would fit, the TV and stereo, the mini refrigerator. I saw and met the girls, loads of them, from schools and towns I'd never heard of, more than enough to go around. All I had to do was stay the course.

A number of my friends and I had been going to stay overnight with college friends for years, often on their homecoming weekend. Not to get brochures or take the tours, but to sneak a taste of all we'd heard about. And what remained were images so vivid they almost itched—what I pictured most when I thought of days to come—and I scratched them frequently. Images of wandering the streets from house to house—the kind in which I hadn't been raised—shabby, roomy, noisy, some packed room to room and floor to floor, most everyone with beers in hand. Whose house it was you couldn't tell, but some of them were known by name. You didn't ask questions. You were just another nameless ripple drifting through a sea of strangers. At times you thought someone might call you out in front of everyone, but no one ever did. The air was warm and ripe with smoke, cologne, and sweat and beer, and voices blended with the music 'til the early morning hours, or until the police showed up.

The schools all seemed the same this way, and the more time passed your past seemed like a flickering bulb that might burn out if you but turned your back on it. Once there you'd start from scratch again, make new and lifelong friends who once they got to know you would give you a nickname that became your new name. And it would be the symbol of that time of so much welcome change. You'd go with the flow and take the path that seemed marked out for you—the path of least resistance, probably—and you'd find that you had worried needlessly. Of course there would be classes too, and homework, but there would be plenty of time for them—if you felt like going, and doing it, that is.

But until then there was work to be done and money to be made, a summer to be drained to the dregs.

# A STRANGE SOLILOQUY

WAS IT RIGHT away, when we first set out to work, or just before leaving for break? The latter is my best guess. Tom and Rudy both heard it and distinctly remember to this day. Funny that we all remember it. Tom was somewhere behind me, and Rudy might have been as well. I was standing between the south corner of the shed and the first-base dugout of Ambrosius, gazing up at the ominous blue-black sky—when unconsciously, half-seriously, my fist rose with my voice in a strange soliloquy:

*Bring it on, Mother Nature!*

Had I siphoned one too many infield lakes? Maybe I was just being my usual silly self. Probably both. Whatever the case, my protest seemed to fall on deaf ears, and we went back to whatever we were on our way to do.

# THERE'S THAT MOMENT

To SAY IT was a dreamlike sort of surreal overwhelming me comes close but far short of describing how it felt—lying there on my back on the damp grass and gravel, staring up at that same deadly sky.

We had only just arrived back at the complex and parked a stone's throw from the shed. We had all just climbed out as usual and began walking that way. For the moment the rain had stopped, and lunch was less than two hours away. Tom and I playfully shoved one another in typical fashion, saying who knows what back and forth. Rudy joined in. He says someone started singing the *Bad Boys* theme song from *Cops*, and he and Tom were suddenly the cops, and I the criminal. A stumbling threefold cord, we jostled and jabbed, got loosely tangled up. With one hand Rudy let go of me to snatch up his cap, which had fallen—or been tossed—into a puddle. We closed in on the ten-foot gap between the shed door and the first-base dugout of Ambrosius, Rudy somewhere on the periphery. Tom and I locked arms and shoulders, throwing our weight around, spinning an unpredictable sort of dance. We slammed against the shed, my back to the wall. A second later we broke apart. I went for his waist, lifting him off his feet for a second. Our momentum shifted in a blur, uncalculated, descending ground-ward irreversibly—I, on the underside, landing buttocks-first, and then the mass of his weight came down on my head, his bulky chest that felt like buttocks, enough to break his fall and force my chin toward my chest. Somehow Rudy, on my right, was still close enough to have a hold of my shirt, as Tom staggered away to the left—both of them still giggling, Rudy recalls.

There was no pain at all. Just a pop and it was over, like snapping the head from a dandelion with your thumb. Just the sound of high-pitched bells I hardly noticed as my eyes beheld my legs—both motionless, one bent at the knee. Just the sight of my right arm falling back at me as quickly as I tried to raise it. Just the fearful words the two beside me couldn't believe: "I can't feel my legs."

Out of sight but less than fifteen feet away, Dan and Chris had just moments before gone into the shed, when they heard a loud voice. Knowing Dan was a premed student, Rudy ran inside and repeated my words. Then, one by one, they came upon us there, more like silhouettes than anything, blank with deer-in-the-headlights wonder.

To think what goes on at any given moment between a person's ears—all we ever see and hear, taste and touch and smell—all passes through the ever-changing veil. To think that every passing thought, perception or conception—hormone sculpted, laden with emotion—becomes a part of us, the fingerprint of who we are, for better or worse. To think that we are all creatures constantly in process, never quite the same from one moment to the next.

There we were, each taking it all in, whatever it was that was happening, this unthinkable thing. And there was the shock, which surely clouded each one differently. Especially the one who lay so still—so unusually still—whose inner systems were all anarchy. He wonders, this one (now, not then), how differently they might have seen it all apart from shock. Would Tom have felt the way you do the instant you've dropped something—a glass while washing dishes, say—and there's that moment where you realize it's too late? You freeze, your mouth half open, watching helplessly the sudden descent. Staring down at the scattered shards between your feet, you think if only I'd reached sooner. Or just the slightest bit to the left. If only. But you didn't. Nor did you have another chance to try. Though, too, you think there may have been no way to reach it, no matter what you did or didn't do. Perhaps the thing was meant to break. Even with the shock it seems this might've crossed his mind. Surely in hindsight it did.

It was Chris who either ran or walked or shuffled nervously in a sort of full-body tremble and dialed those three notorious numbers no one can forget. The only phone on the grounds, a pay phone, was attached to the outside wall of the concession stand, its last four digits 9923—Wayne Gretzky-Michael Jordan, we always said—which would ring and ring and ring some days when one of the higher-ups had a special message to relay from downtown, a certain task or errand for us, and at least two of us, no matter how far away we were, would drop whatever we were doing and sprint for it as if the fate of the world were at stake. And though it wasn't ringing there and then, to some degree the future of each one there did hang in the balance.

Waiting what felt to them like hours for the sirens, these comrades sat around me in silence. Without anyone, even myself, noticing—without even knowing himself why he did it—Rudy yanked a small patch of hair out of one of my very hairy legs, noting that I didn't flinch an inch. And soon enough the flashing lights and uniforms arrived with their unsurprised demeanor, their calm and easy questions, talking us through everything they did. They put a C-collar around my neck to hold it still, rolled me onto the long backboard, then to the stretcher, then into the big white womb on wheels. It is all one blurry moment in my mind's eye, like gazing into a raindrop in your hand.

Sometime after we left, the boss arrived. He almost never came to the complex, unless maybe he was in the neighborhood or had something to bring us. I imagine the guys were a little nervous, though probably also pretty numb. But he just brought them into the shed and they sat down and explained as best they could. And when it started to rain again they were sent home for the day, to wonder what it all might mean in the end.

The next day they returned like any other day, but probably it was not like any other day. Did they still shoot Rock, Paper, Scissors for jobs? Did they still race for the phone if it rang? Maybe some of them wondered if it hadn't just been in their heads, a kind of morbid scenario they had concocted while lost in thought, and now they were back to their senses again, and though there was this unmistakable feeling they couldn't shake which made them feel as though the ground beneath them might give way at any moment, before long Ted would pull up in his navy-blue Mercury and join them for another day, carefree as ever, and life would feel the way it felt before.

# A KIND OF SECOND
# NATURE BEHAVIOR

IT WAS SOMETHING you had taken for granted from childhood, as though it were part of what defined you as a male. Risky and dangerous were not the kind of words you associated with this kind of casual give and take. After all, there were school wrestling and football and hockey programs, where kids routinely slammed into one another and crushed each other to the ground, the applause of teachers, peers, and parents cheering them on. It wasn't as though you hadn't heard your parents warn you countless times over the years to be careful when "roughhousing" (their word) this way. But, of course, you always shrugged them off without a second thought, convinced you'd be okay—and usually you were—that you were the captain of your destiny from one moment to the next, and day by day and year by year this resolution fossilized into a state of mind and heart that came to rule your ways.

And before you knew it, there you were, alert but discombobulated, a crumpled heap of humbled flesh and bones. A masterpiece of irony—at a fork in the road, without a choice to make. You'd made your choices, and the rest was out of your hands.

The drawn-out days would come when you would wonder how your choices led to this. The choices of *that* day especially, but also every day that came before. Even those of others that touched your life. And that's not all you'd wonder as you wandered through the wilderness of Why, compelled by a deep and burning urge to know—w*hy this, why now, why me*? *Why not some other fate?* Like the time my fifth-grade buddy, Craig, and I hiked more than a mile along some lonely creek, and he crashed through the ice and I somehow fished him out, and shivering we staggered home in the falling snow? Why not from flying off the road—that narrow country road, in that tiny car—without a seatbelt at ninety miles an hour? Why not the handful of times I drove home drunk? Why, a week or so before that day, as I stood on the railroad tracks above Ravine Lake and watched the firebrands younger than me dare to dive, did something stronger than pride make me think twice?

This was where the fork invariably led—this kind of constant questioning—the road you had and hadn't chosen. You couldn't blame the road alone, and yet you couldn't help but ask. And because you saw no other road to take, you tried to grin and bear it with a smile. And it worked sometimes, and you inched along. But more than sometimes questions without answers took their toll. And in the end that restless road was only a dead end.

# THE REST OF THE MORNING

I<small>T WAS THE</small> same hospital in which I had come screaming into the world eighteen years earlier, where I now lay much larger and lankier, though equally helpless. I suppose that first day of my life brought inexplicable joy and awe into my parents' hearts and minds as they gazed upon my vulnerable little frame. Since then I had never broken a bone or sustained any kind of really debilitating injury, let alone being admitted as an inpatient. I did have friends, though, who had. When we were fourteen, my close friend John fell off his old quarter-horse, Reese Honey, which left him with a punctured lung and broken ribs. And then, the summer before our senior year, another childhood blood-brother had to have his jaw broken and reset, which meant that for weeks afterward he was forced to suck down meals through a straw. Both were temporarily subject to hospital beds and the humility that comes with that experience. But as grave as their circumstances seemed to me as I stood at their respective bedsides, with time each of them gradually recovered and returned to their normal selves, more or less. A year later you'd never know they'd had such experiences.

My parents were told at work—Mom by phone and Dad in person—that their son had been in a serious accident and they needed to get to the hospital as soon as possible. As you might imagine, they didn't know what to think but simply did as they were told. My sister got the call at home from Tom. When he told her, she matter-of-factly called his bluff, suspecting a prank, as my buddies and I might well be suspected. But he persisted, assuring her as gravely as he could that it was no joke and she needed to get to the hospital immediately.

The X-ray revealed a "subluxation"—or shifting out of place—of the fifth and sixth cervical vertebra. This meant increasing swelling of the spinal cord moment by moment, though surprisingly a series of checkboxes on the ER record notes my demeanor as "calm," "alert," "quiet," "cooperative," and "oriented"—not to mention one other interesting detail handwritten above the others: "tan." Apparently I made it known that I'd heard my neck crack and was unable to move my legs, and that I was eighteen and right-handed. Weak traces of movement remained in my hands and arms, but my sensations and reflexes, as well as ability to grasp, were negative. A Foley catheter was inserted, and a corticosteroid given to address the pain and swelling I don't remember feeling.

When my parents and sister were sent in, I looked up at them and said something to the effect that my wallet was in my car back at work, and they would need to make sure to stop by and pick it up. I told them not to worry about me, that everything would be okay. My sister, however, maintains that I looked "so scared." But she remembers little else, except taking hold of my hand and saying she loved me, which I apparently reciprocated. Dad remembers the pastor of our church holding my hand the whole time. Mom recalls that I was, at one point, screaming in pain. But that's about all we've been able to piece together of that particular scene. Otherwise, all I can say is that when I try to imagine what I might have been thinking and feeling if I had been standing where they were and one of them had been lying in front of me in such a condition, I instantly tear up.

Before long it was decided that I would need to be airlifted to Sioux Falls. But by that time the midday skies were nearly black, and the region was under both a severe thunderstorm and tornado warning. This made leaving immediately out of the question, even though time was of the essence in preventing the swelling from causing any further damage. But as everyone waited out the agonizing minutes that followed, a few desperate prayers must have prevailed, because by mid-afternoon the flight was given clearance. But not before our assistant pastor gave Dad a quick ride home to change clothes and pack a suitcase, after which they stopped briefly on the way to the airport to lock up Dad's shop, which he'd left open in his rush to the hospital. When they arrived at the airport, it seems the initial plan was to use a helicopter to fly around the storm, but since one wasn't available the only option was a plane that for some reason was still in the air, which had to be landed immediately. In addition to the pilot and myself, Dad was joined by two nurses, as the plane first headed straight west to Miller to sidestep the storm, then swung back southeast for Sioux Falls.

Meanwhile, Mom hurried back to the flower shop to set things in order with her employees for the following day, packed a suitcase of her own, and hitched a ride with one of her dearest friends. In the midst of this whirlwind, Sarah was left behind, though she wound up catching a ride with Tom. Mom says Connie kept things on the lighter side, which helped, and neither Sarah nor Tom remembers much about the drive, except that they listened without speaking to Radiohead's new album as they stared down the vacant prairie landscape, bleeding their silent streams of tears.

Sometimes there are just no words to be said. You want to say something, anything that might put you or someone else at ease. But it's no use. You hunt for what to say but find nothing. These are not times for finding words, let alone the right words. They are times for music or silence—or even, strangely, sometimes laughter—for tears and hugs and prayers and sleep.

# MEANWHILE

Around town my friends were hearing the news one-by-one as word spread, which took longer in those days before the all-pervasive reign of cell phone and Internet. By late afternoon a lot of them were gathering over at the house of one of my best friends, whose parents were both doctors and as such would know the latest concerning my status. It was still early and people were hearing different things, so no one was really sure what to make of it all. It was serious, they knew that much and were quite taken aback, but what did that really mean? Normally we all hung out in the basement, where the pool table was, but that afternoon they were all in the family room, upstairs, adult territory. And at some point in the midst of what was apparently a little too casual conversation and perhaps even joking, a familiar but unexpectedly stern voice—the voice of a father, the ophthalmologist, with his unmistakable Indian accent—suddenly broke like a clap of thunder through the room. This was not just an ordinary day, he began, and this was no time for lighthearted banter. Their good friend was never going to be the same again, and they had better let that sink in.

# SIOUX VALLEY

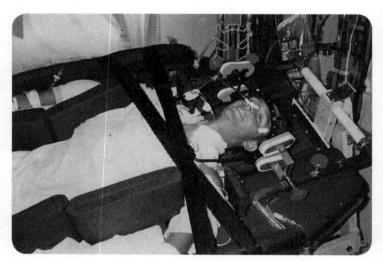

Sioux Valley, the Stryker frame bed

# A VERY UNFORTUNATE GENTLEMAN

FOR SOME REASON I had gone to Sioux Falls with my Aunt Norma to pick up a load of something I don't quite remember that we had filling the back seat of her little blue Volkswagen Fox. Oddly, the only image I have is of a large stash of hard liquor, but I'm not sure how that could have been so (I was just seventeen). Anyway, before we left town she allowed me to stop by Sioux Valley Hospital to visit my close buddy Craig, who had just had his jaw broken and reset. I remember being dropped off out front to the right of the entrance and strolling carefree through the lobby, unprepared. The room itself was fairly dark, though it was the middle of the afternoon, and his mom might or might not have been sitting somewhere in the shadows. The head of his bed was raised to a semi-sitting position, he appeared semi-sedated, and the few things he managed to say were through clenched teeth. I had never seen anyone, let alone my usually good-humored pal, look so grim. It was a brief but sobering few minutes that really made me think and feel for him.

A year or so later, on my second visit there—which really was not a visit—I entered not through the lobby on foot but through the bowels of the building on a gurney. Of which moments I remember nothing. I only know by a little detective work that it was about mid-afternoon when the plane touched down safely at the airport and a waiting ambulance rushed me to the emergency room. An MRI was given, and within an hour and a half I was in intensive care with my parents being briefed by the doctor as we waited for space in the OR. Another hour and a half would pass in pre-op, and then another hour and a half until surgery began.

So much is blur the further back you go, especially those first two weeks—or four or six or eight. What's clear is clear, yet even what's not still clings as if it won't be left behind. And clear or not, you always have to ask yourself if it's memory or dream you think you recall. Like the ride in the plane—strapped to a gurney covered in white as sudden flashes of light occasionally filled the small black oval windows, Dad close by my side. Or those fleeting moments as I lay alone in the silence of some twilight room—in pre-op probably, who knows which time—still covered in blankets white and warm and staring nowhere in particular—the fragile moment fear took hold. First and foremost fear of where I was and what I was doing there; that something dreadful lay ahead, and I had no choice or way to help myself. There seemed one option: close your eyes and resign to whatever might come, whatever that might mean. At the very least it meant a part of me would die right there and then. The first—without my knowing it—of a series of similar deaths to come.

Three hours later, surgery was over, and an hour after that Mom and Dad heard the doctor say that things went well, though prognosis still uncertain. And before they left, near midnight, they were allowed a quick peek in at their son, who seemed to be resting well despite the sterile spider web of wires and tubes attached to him—the most conspicuous the large one down his throat. They had finally reached the end of what had been a long and grueling first day, and more details were probably the last thing they had the wherewithal to bear. It was enough for them to see their firstborn lying there half-alive in what appeared to be a semblance of peace and quiet. He'd survived, and they could breathe again. Better than the alternative. There'd be time in days to come to process all and hope together for the best. After all, there is a time for everything, as savvy Solomon once proclaimed.

In time we all learned more than we ever cared to know about quadriplegia. Sometimes it takes time to learn, years even, and there are no shortcuts or substitutes, for which on occasion you are surprised to find yourself thankful. We learned that my spinal cord had been at least partially severed, causing paralysis from the chest down—the diagnosis: quadriplegia, which, as the name implies, affects both arms and legs. We learned that the damage I sustained is what they call "complete," meaning a total loss of sensory and motor function below the break. We learned that an injury at C5-6 allows a person some control of the head, neck, shoulders, arms, and hands, but not the abdominal muscles or diaphragm, which makes breathing and especially coughing more difficult. It's also the level at which some manner of self-care becomes possible, as well as the prospect of privileges like pushing a manual wheelchair or driving a car with adaptive equipment. Not that anyone was looking that far ahead.

It's amazing to comb through the reams of records and try to decipher (with Google's help) the technical tale of all they'd been doing to me—oblivious me. You read of the application of Gardener-Wells tongs, and removal of herniated, nucleated pulposus, and open reduction of subluxation of C5 on C6, and anterior interbody fusion of C5-6 with a #25 Synthes plate, and application of halo vest and frame, and posterior fusion of C5-6 with interspinuous wiring right C5 facet to C6 spinous process wiring, and bone graft from iliac crest. Pages and pages, two inches thick. But fortunately here and there this jargon gives way to plain English, beginning with things like the nuts and bolts basics of biography and family health history. Including how exactly the injury occurred, the details slightly different in each doctor's report. More than once the young man is referred to in different turns of phrase as "a very unfortunate gentleman," the thesis statement standing out amid all the procedural mumbo-jumbo.

The initial surgeries and procedures all happened within a few days. A second surgery was needed on the second day to make an adjustment to a slight shift in the fusion between vertebra that resulted from the application of the halo apparatus to my skull and upper torso. A shard of bone had actually been removed from my hip to aid in this fusion. Had I known what was going on, I might've wondered what all the fuss was over a few millimeters of shifting spine. Who knew a millimeter mattered so much? But life had entered a new realm where minutia not only matters, it matters infinitely. A simple clot of blood bridges the gulf between life and death. So that by the time I finish browsing the stack of old medical reports, noting how many fronts of the battle there were, and how intense, I have to wonder how I even survived the first few hours. Which makes me ponder further that if there were only some way for us all to know the degree to which our fragile frames of flesh and soul are continually sustained from one moment to the next, how stupefied and humbled we should be. Then maybe one could hope that nearly every breath and heartbeat might be more deeply treasured as the momentary miracles they are.

And so, to keep the wonder of my freshly fused spine fixed firmly for recovery, the halo was necessary. The device that looked like something out of a medieval torture chamber, which in the same spirit was literally screwed into my skull in four places—one above each eyebrow and behind each ear—making it impossible to turn my head one way or the other. One glimpse revealed the origin of its name—the narrow band of metal that encircles the skull, hovering just above the eyebrows. To this thick band are fastened four rods about a foot long each, which are secured to a solid plastic shoulder harness that encloses the upper torso, with something like lambswool to protect the skin from the plastic. So whenever several times a day they rolled me on my side I felt as though I were inside a see-through box, more like a piece of furniture than flesh. And some of my closest buddies, bold as they thought they were, would wilt at the sight, or even just walking through those solemn hallways. With time most everyone adjusted, though, while some never made it even once. And you couldn't blame them. I wasn't exactly a pretty sight. Still, there were family and friends who came that very first day, then on and off throughout the weeks thereafter, sometimes half a dozen to more than a dozen a day.

Life before June 29 seemed to come and go so easily, and there seemed to be so few limitations in my daily schedule. Plans often changed on a whim. I might decide to stand or sit or walk or run; might climb the stairs, hop in the car, make angels in the snow; might leave town or stay the night with friends; might water-ski, play basketball, go hunting, mow the lawn. Now the boundaries had narrowed considerably: one city, one building, one neighborhood; one floor, one wing, one room, one single bed. Sleeping, waking, eating, drinking, bathing, grooming, pooping, peeing, stretching, you name it—happened in bed.

In a single moment life had been transformed from an active state of almost constant, spontaneous independence to a completely inactive, dependent, even more constant haze, where the distinction between dreams and reality had become virtually indistinguishable. The kind of transitory bedlam in which it was not unusual to feel your legs like long balloons floating five feet above you in bed, with just your neck and shoulders still touching—the fallout of heavy anesthesia, impaired breathing, random cycles of sleeping and waking. Pneumonia came and went, and every few days they'd suck the mucus from my lungs. IV antibiotics followed, and a feeding tube, a ventilator back in for the second surgery, then removed, then back in a few days later when I lost strength and needed blood. All this in the bed that slowly back-and-forth would rotate all day long, blood clots and bedsores being the greatest threats to bed-bound life. And that much more since all the plump and creamy bags of meals could not keep up with the steadily disappearing pounds—from a hundred-fifty to a hundred in just two months. Sometimes I was with it enough to talk, but usually I slept through most visitors.

The rooms themselves were small, cookie-cutter clones of one another, each enclosed by its own set of sliding-glass doors and curtains, machines aplenty ever beeping, sighing, everywhere a wire or tube, or monitor or television flashing, day or night; voices, faces, familiar, unfamiliar, male, female, faintly chatting, whispering, coming, going, asking you what day or month or year it is; stealing blood, measuring this, cleaning that, at all hours nudging you, turning you every which way as you shivered, one moment, and the next broke into sweat. This and a thousand details more for the forward-looking one who, like his sister, never napped as a kid, wild with ambition from the womb, for whom patience had never been a virtue. For this reason one could almost be thankful—if one were conscious enough—for this bewildering blur.

# ALL THE DIFFERENCE

IT CERTAINLY WOULD not have been my first choice of daunting challenges through which to persevere, if somehow I'd been given the choice and chance, like some perverse reality show. And yet I probably couldn't have picked a better place to pass that time, where I was waited on around the clock like royalty, by faithful hearts and hands who, though they didn't know me, tenderly scratched my every itch and cleaned up my vilest messes. Who'd pin a call light near my hand or chin, and all I had to do was give a push—though that wasn't always so easy as you'd think— and in they'd come, for anything at all, even popsicles at two a.m.

Sometimes I wonder how I might have fared a hundred years ago. FDR's wooden wheelchair springs to mind. And that wasn't even a hundred years ago, depending how you count. Maybe they would have put me away in some asylum with a bunch of others like me and treated us who knows how. If I survived the injury itself, that is. In some countries, maybe even America, they might have put me down right there on the spot, like a wounded horse. That might have seemed to them the more humane thing. There would be no X-rays, MRIs, or EKGs to offer, nor rotating beds, electric wheelchairs, easy antibiotics. It's hard to believe that in so many countries that situation still hasn't changed. Amazing what a hundred years can mean—for some. Or to think that when and where you were born, to say nothing of to whom, could mean so much—could mean all the difference in the world.

# WHAT YOU DO SOMETIMES

WHEN YOUR MEDS have been reduced enough that the haze which once enveloped you no longer shields you from the conscious world. When your visitors and nurse's aides have left you to yourself, and you've had enough TV, and you're pretty sure you've taken stock of every last thing in the room, from the multiplied decorations to the hideous suction container and sphygmomanometer. When you've even taken the time to figure out—syllable by syllable—exactly how to pronounce *sphyg-mo-man-o-met-er*. Then is when you find yourself beginning to count the square-foot ceiling tiles. First length, then width, then double-check, then multiply. Then add the partial panels in. Then, squinting, gaze more closely, try your best to do the same with the tiny checkerboard of holes that fill each square. Two tries convinces you you're done. And just when you think you've had enough, you suddenly start to recite your

ABCs—in sections, slowly, with the melody, taking your time. And then, with a quirky smile, you keep the tune but change it up—Z-Y-X-W-V-U-T; S-R-Q-P-O-N-M; L-K-J, I-H-G; F-E-D and C-B-A. Repeated like a mantra 'til it's just as easy as the normal way, a pointless skill that's still with you today.

You ponder how much different things might be without TV, without your friends or family ever there. You know deep down you have no right to complain, that some have it unspeakably worse. And yet with the way you've been brought up, a product of the time and place you didn't choose, you naturally tend to take for granted every last extravagance.

Sometimes you almost totally forget why you're lying there and wonder why you aren't up and around, going and doing like everyone else. You look down at your crumpled hands, at rest on either side of your blanket-covered legs. With your mind you squeeze them tightly into fists, relax, then squeeze again. Then stretch your fingers all the way out, then wiggle them up and down in sequence like a rolling wave. You feel them burning, tingling, actually doing what you command, but they don't flinch an inch. You do it with your toes too. Your ankles, knees, and hips—raise them up and down, back and forth, together, separately, twist and flex them vigorously. It almost wears you out, trying so hard. You imagine a baseball in your hand—the familiar feel of leather and the stitches, the different grips for different pitches. Then a tennis racket—steady swings of forehand, backhand, follow-through. You grit your teeth and try to will your shriveled torso up, your head and neck strained forward off the pillow an inch or so—one, two, three, four, five seconds—and your head falls back again with a sigh. Then bounces back up as you grunt and close your eyes, give it everything you have, never more willing, imagining and feeling both your legs swing off the bed, planted firmly on the cold tile floor, heat and pressure rushing down as you lean your weight on them. Again your head drops back with a heavy sigh as you glance down at your hands and legs. You wonder how you ever did any of it before, even brushing your teeth or lifting a fork. You figure you must have been a walking miracle—one marvelous miracle after the next.

# LOOKING UP

By MID-AUGUST THAT cozy room in the ICU had grown into a shrine of sentiments. Balloons and flowers, T-shirts, cards, framed pictures of my friends and me, on every ledge or tray-on-wheels; small plaques with boldfaced words like *Courage*, *Patience*, *Strength*, *Believe*. As soon as someone learned I had a favorite this or that, another care package would arrive—Gummy Lifesavers and Rolos came the most, first one by one then by the bag. A few buddies chipped in for a portable CD player. The familiar crew from the ball fields smuggled in a beloved "cocoon" from the Donut Shoppe. Another close friend and his parents even splurged for a VCR. One evening I laughed so hard at the only movie I remember seeing—*Uncle Buck*, with John Candy—that I could scarcely breathe, which set off my heart monitor and sent a nurse rushing into the room.

Things were finally starting to look up a bit. A month and a half in that rotating bed hadn't completely prevented pressure sores, but the ones that did form were superficial and nearly healed. The mind-numbing haze from the pain meds was also gone. Slight increases in weight and stamina meant the end of tube feedings and the transition to being fed by mouth. When Uncle Bryce and Aunt Marge came to visit, they loved bringing in chocolate shakes from Fuddruckers (they seemed to take as much delight in bringing them as I did in devouring them). My deltoids and left bicep had also strengthened, and I was even beginning to tolerate sitting up in a wheelchair, though at first only a few minutes at a time, due to dizziness. But the rehab team seemed to think I was stable enough to benefit from a plan for "increasing functional independence," which meant I'd be transferring to the rehab floor.

Up to that point, the PTs came to the room to stretch whatever it is they stretched. It was mostly my wrists and ankles, I think, though likely also my arms and shoulders, which frequently ached. When the time came to roll my bed down the hallway and they got me laid out on their padded table, it was more intense and included my legs. I don't remember what all OT had me working on, probably trying to use the little grasp I had to pick up, with one or both hands, an assortment of blocks or pegs or playing cards, then to transfer them to some receptacle. Speech therapy, I remember, consisted mainly of inhaling as deeply as I could into a plastic device in which lay a small cylinder of white plastic, which would hover in the air as long as I held that breath. The goal was to make it reach a certain blue line, which took many tries and much brass-headed resolve.

In the meantime, the visitors kept coming, less than before but still coming. Many were familiar, but there were also some I either didn't know at all or only vaguely remembered, friends of my parents or the moms or dads of friends or classmates of mine. Some brought homemade casseroles or cookies and just sat down for a while to talk. Before leaving they'd touch my arm or kiss my forehead, standing there silently with eyes that said it all.

When I got up to rehab, one regular visitor was a grandfatherly chaplain named Rev. Brack. At least once a week he'd pop in and chat a little, then read a devotion with me and pray. He had a classic chaplain demeanor, which I think of as quiet and dignified. He had sort of a raspy voice, white hair, rosy face, large-framed glasses, and gold-rimmed teeth. It cheered you just to see him walk in, always smiling. Years later, I decided to share with him by letter how thankful I was for those visits. Writing back, he explained how he had read my letter just before leaving for a meeting with a group of his fellow chaplains, who were gathering to discuss whether or not the chaplain services at the hospital were worth continuing. So off he went with my letter in hand, which he took to be unmistakable evidence of the will of God on the matter.

It still amazes me that Mom and Dad somehow managed to alternate making the two-hour one-way drives each week, despite their busy work schedules and having my sister to look after. Mom came Sunday through Thursday, leaving her shop in the hands of faithful coworkers, and Dad closed his shop to relieve her Thursday through the weekend. A couple of Mom's old softball friends happened to live in Sioux Falls, one of whom had a spare bedroom, which saved them oodles on lodging over those months. But once their days with me were done, it was straight back home to catch up on another hectic half-week, all the while playing the part-time single parent.

One of the sweeter memories of my time on the rehab floor is of Mom or Dad almost daily pulling up a chair beside my bed and opening the piles of mail that poured in. Before opening each one they would first announce who it was from, then slowly and sincerely read them aloud, whether just a few words or multiplied paragraphs. If there was booty inside, they would hold up each item up for me to see, and we would smile or laugh, or occasionally shed a tear. The neighbor girl who lived at the end of our street, a friend and classmate of mine from childhood, faithfully wrote me from college nearly every week. We always looked forward to her letters, which were full of energy and life. Thanks, Mris. Those letters meant more than you might have guessed.

# HEALING

SARAH CAME TO visit one day while I was on the rehab floor. She probably visited other times, but this one I remember in particular. She was alone, if I'm remembering correctly. She sat in a chair on the right-hand side of my bed, the room bright white with light. For some reason the memory carries the idea that she was in college, but that's impossible. She wasn't yet seventeen. It was a short, sweet visit. There was a moment when we both had tears in our eyes. I don't remember anything we said, except maybe "I love you." I don't know what it was like to see what she saw from where she was sitting. I don't know what that does to a sister—the only sister of an only brother—especially at that age. All I know is that any bad blood that might have been between us as brother and sister was forever washed under the bridge after that.

# IMAGINE HIS SURPRISE

*YOU'RE NOT GOING to walk again*, I can barely still hear her saying as she left the room.

One of the nurse's aides, who—bless her soul—was either having a bad day or perhaps had had enough of the naive optimism of her young patient. More than just his frequent smiles, or his just as frequent upbeat ways of saying, "I'm fine, things are fine." Probably it was more his talk of walking again someday. It's hard to say how much he actually said, or what it was exactly that brought it on. Maybe she thought it cruel to postpone what seemed inevitable and felt an obligation to respond. And if that's how it was, you could hardly blame her. After all, you can imagine how reluctant those closest to him probably felt about having to break such news. Maybe they thought there would come a right time for it. Or maybe all his smiling and positivity made them think that he was starting to embrace the fact on his own. In reality the lens through which he processed that long season generally took a glass-half-full approach and, like a rearview mirror, bent it into more than just half-full. Somehow it helped him feel that he was merely bouncing back from something like the flu or chickenpox. It was a kind of working assumption he gradually began taking for granted without thinking much about it. All he seemed to know is that clearly something had happened, and he was recovering, and soon he'd be off again before he knew it to life as usual—even college, after all this interruption.

So imagine his surprise when, swallowing hard, a double stream of tears burned down his cheeks. The thought had never hit him so squarely. It may seem strange, but such was the nature of that lens—the kind through which we're all content to see the world at times, when waking up to what we know deep down is just too much. It stung and left a welt and throbbed, and all he could do was let it have its way. And soon the guy from psych stopped in to ask how things were going, and of course he answered as he thought he felt, that things were fine and he was fine, and then there was another sting and welt and throb, and then another question suddenly: "Then why are you crying?" To which he had no answer, only more and more unruly tears. And what he felt was something like the bygone days when older cousins pinned him down and pounded on his forehead endlessly. Or the time he fell face first, exhausted, through the finish line, and the crowd (his Dad there

also) cried, "Oh!" as he fought back the tears. Like it or
not, he was forced to say "uncle"—no way to save face. The
kind of giving in that almost lacks the wherewithal to cry.
Almost—for just when he thought he'd hit the bottom, it
wasn't long before his mom confessed—as tenderly as she
knew how—that he wouldn't be going to college in the fall.

# CODE BLUE

It might have been my second week in rehab. Dad was visiting that day and had just stepped outside for some fresh air. When he returned, I was gone, and they told him why.

I was sprawled out on the physical therapy table for routine stretching when things went suddenly black. A moment later my eyes were slowly opening as from sleep to a clear mask over my nose and mouth, and a couple of paramedics kneeling over me. That's the last thing I remember. I'm glad Dad wasn't there. Especially when they started CPR—and when that didn't take, the electric paddles. But first they had to remove the halo. I'm glad I wasn't there either.

Mom got the call at work. She dropped everything, drove home, packed a bag, and within an hour was out the door to catch a ride with Uncle Lyle. Sarah says she was home at the time, but neither she nor Mom recalls whether she came along. Dad eventually found his way to the chaplain and, in his words, "went to pieces"—three days before their anniversary.

The doctors called it a pulmonary embolism, or a blood clot in the lung, which had traveled up from one of my legs and caused my heart to stop. I don't know how long it took to bring me back. But before they knew it I was gone again, and another round of CPR was followed with the paddles one last time. Which worked, but then pneumonia settled in. Then back downstairs to the ICU and another ventilator down my throat—and another feeding tube through my nose, and a week of chest X-rays I don't remember, two or three times a day, apparently, for the first few days. I remember the room—not the same as the first I'd had—and which way my bed was facing, Mom and Dad's somber faces in the doorway, the helpless feeling of no voice (the first time I was with it enough to tell). To tell them what I needed— even just a simple drink of water—meant they had to read my eyes, and choose their questions well. I could only look intently, nodding yes or shaking no. And I imagine they were probably wondering if that was going to be my final stand.

I remember the rawness of my throat the day they pulled the ventilator out, but that was better than having it in. All therapy ceased. The hours and days kept stumbling by. And in the clearest moments in the silence after dark, the future loomed unwritten and ghastly, like a childhood monster lurking around the bend.

# GOOD RIDDANCE

THE RECORDS SAY it was the last week of September when the halo finally came off for good—the day before I was readmitted to rehab. Sometimes it's tricky reconciling the records with the memories. It's hard to think of that long stay in stages or phases. Most of the distinctions seem to be marked more by what month it was, or what room I was in or floor I was on. Until the records set me straight, I didn't realize I still had the halo on during the Code Blue.

I distinctly remember being in the ICU when it came off, the head of the bed fully inclined, a few friends standing around watching. I was actually a little surprised and unnerved that it could be removed while you were fully conscious, and before an audience. I imagine what now seems an interesting side note didn't occur to any of us then, that the removal of the thing might have been seen as symbolic of the transition, in the way of those creatures that shed and leave behind their creepy exoskeletons. A little curious, I Google it and find that it is arthropods (spiders, reptiles, etc.) that perform this feat—*ecdysis*, from the Greek ἐκδύω (*ekduo*), "to take off, strip off"—which allows a creature to grow. What's left behind is called the *exuvia*, a Latin word meaning "that which is stripped from a body." Interesting. For several years this creepy "exoskeleton" hung in Mom and Dad's garage, but now it resides in some lonely shed out in the country, I know not why.

So the good doctor set to work on me, though there wasn't much work to it. Just a matter of loosening the screws and lifting the thing away without causing too much discomfort as the final millimeters of the screws simultaneously emerged from their holes, biting slightly. It reminds me of getting my braces off after two years when I was sixteen, though that freedom pales in comparison. I can imagine but don't remember moving my head back and forth and up and down ever so slowly, lost in the moment, awed by the simple pleasure. Three months, it had been. One more privilege taken for granted. If you look closely enough, you can still see the scars above my eyebrows. Sometimes when I'm dizzy or laughing a lot the ones behind my ears sort of ache, and for some reason it feels better if I take my glasses off a minute. The other battle scars it left are only seen by those who help me shower. I've never even seen them. It was the massive weight loss in conjunction with certain conspicuous parts of the frame, which dug deep enough holes in my shoulder blades to require skin grafts.

There were other procedures too, once I got up to rehab. Within a week of the skin grafts they put in a suprapubic catheter site about three inches below my bellybutton—a permanently indwelling tube that needs to be changed every two to three weeks. Excessive kidney stones, apparently, had been a problem, and somehow this was supposed to help. I remember bouts of migraine madness, desperate groans for mercy through clenched teeth. As always, there was a term for it: *autonomic dysreflexia*—which is the body's way of telling you, like an infant wailing, something's wrong.

I remember trying to brush my teeth and wash my face and feed myself, but still needing full assistance. After so many months in bed and so much strength and dexterity lost (though I'd also gained some back in increments), it didn't take much to become fatigued. I remember the frustration of needing that assistance, having to ask for nearly everything because I was still unable on my own. Half the battle is in the simple admission of the fact. It's a true pride killer. I also remember getting in the wheelchair more, but the records say I could only get my hand to the joystick half the time. Eventually, though, I got strong enough to drive myself to therapy and back, which sometimes felt like riding a rodeo bronc, herky-jerky as some of those old chairs were. I even discovered that I could give hugs, which I gave every chance I got.

# YOU'LL HAVE TO LEARN

"YOU'LL HAVE TO learn," is what he says she told him—a woman who looked like she might know—when he asked how he and his wife should care for their son, once they got him home.

For example, how should he be lifted? How to help him do the hundred things being done for him in there each day? The careful stretching, bathing, dressing, toileting. Maybe his question shot forth like a reflex, along the lines of, "How in the world are we supposed to do all this?"

They had done it all before, of course, when the kid was so much smaller. They didn't need special advice then. There were questions, as there always are, but mostly things came naturally. But what to do for one grown up so much, perhaps not even finished growing yet? They'd casually watched these cares for months, and yet whoever thought one day they would need to know themselves? Even early on they never thought the stay would last so long. They half-expected him to walk again.

*You'll have to learn.*

*You'll have to learn.*

*You'll have to learn.*

I wonder if that didn't reverberate through his mind for days afterward.

"Well, how do I do that?" was his response, to which he might or might not have received the same answer. Here was a guy who, like his wife, would rip out his still-beating heart for his kids. And yet this simple answer stopped him cold. Was he thinking back on days when he himself had known a change of course, when an engine suddenly dropped onto his chest from the car under which he lay? (I recall the brace he wore for years—perhaps still wore—and as a kid lying next to him on the carpet as he stretched his legs.) Desire didn't matter here. Facts were facts—one in particular: his broken back. Besides, he was fifty-nine and still at work; his wife the same, not far behind at fifty-two.

To bring him home is all they wanted. Six months in there was long enough. But a home without a wheelchair ramp or lift, or ready shifts of twenty-four-hour staff? And what of all the costs? And if they couldn't do it, then who would? A nursing home or group home, where he might lie unattended for hours on end, and share his room with a senile stranger hollering who knows what?

Years later, friends and family sometimes asked, "How did you get through it all?" To which they've often said, "You do what you have to do." More often, though, they also add, "Our faith in God is what got us through."

# HOME,
# BITTERSWEET HOME

# HOME

I WAS AS surprised as anyone to be lying there in the driveway, looking back up into my empty wheelchair, wondering where I'd gone. It was a mild summer evening, I'd been home about six months, and the guys and I were getting in late, possibly after a wedding dance. Most of us were three sheets to the wind, and after I'd made a couple haphazard figure-eights in the street and looped back to the top of the driveway, closest the garage, one of the guys hopped on back. It was a trick we had fun repeating, which we had discovered unexpectedly one day when one of them happened to stand on my wheelie bars as I gave it full throttle and we rode a pavement-scraping wheelie for ten or fifteen feet, laughing all the way. But that was usually on a level surface in broad daylight, with our wits (however dim) about us. In this case we barely reached the middle of the (declining) driveway, which meant my hand must have slipped off the joystick, bringing the chair to a sudden stop (a built-in safety feature, incidentally). And these were the days before I'd learned the benefits of a seatbelt—that might've been the very lesson that taught me, in fact—so the guys found themselves scrambling to peel me off the pavement and reload me as quickly as possible. And just when they got me back in and headed up the ramp, I nearly drove off the open side of it, one of the guys catching my front wheel and leg rest just in time.

You could blame it on booze or immaturity, but at the end of the day it spelled the beginning of letting go (the wrong kind). Which in this case left me in the awkward position of the next day having to explain away things like the still-bloody three-inch gash in my forearm. I said I had caught it between the armrest of my chair and the jamb of the front garage door entrance—through which my bulky chair didn't even fit—and Mom and Dad seemed to buy it hook, line, and sinker, though they and the nurses probably had their suspicions. I imagine from time to time they wondered if that kind of late night *gallivanting* (their word) was going to be the norm for the months to come. After all, hadn't they just graduated that one and felt the relief of knowing there was just one more left at home to keep track of? If they did have anxiety, they didn't show it—though I wouldn't have been the one to notice. But for all they knew, I might have wound up staying there indefinitely, though that prospect never crossed my mind. It probably would've terrified me, and maybe them too.

Those seven months slipped by so quietly. Looking back, they seem more like a few weeks than months. Especially in the days just after I returned, when the nearly nonstop stream of friends and family flocked to the house for days on end, to wish us all a welcome home and Happy New Year. When all was golden, so many possibilities, though it took a while to settle in. It took a while to even believe I was actually there and not lost in just another half-conscious figment of dreamland, where what seemed true to life might the next moment dissolve into the same old room back on the rehab floor. But everything seemed too much like it always had, from the moment we turned down Lampert Drive for the first time since the injury to the slight bend just before the same old blood-red house with brick and white trim. That is, all but the large *Welcome Home* banner hanging below the living room window. Sure enough, behind the wintry windows, one by one the joyful smiles eventually appeared. Nothing dissolved. It was home after all.

Home, where so many were not just stopping by but eagerly and frequently offering themselves to help in one way and another—many who only knew me as Dick and Lila's boy. Several fundraisers were organized in those short months to help offset some of the costs Mom and Dad had been steadily incurring. The first was an auction/pork feed, spearheaded by my Aunt Dee and a close family friend, Jerry Micheel. Then my buddy Tom's forty-eight-year-old dad came out of retirement as an amateur rodeo rider to offer "A Few Bucks for Ted," to which people and businesses donated based on how many seconds he could ride a bull (amazingly, he lasted six). After that there was a basketball game between a handful of hometown personalities and a Sioux Falls TV sports anchor (and former Huron High School basketball starter) and his team of news celebrities. And by the end of summer Mom even got a bunch of her old softball cronies together for a game of underhand fast pitch. Together, they raised over ten thousand dollars, though the amount paled in comparison with the spirit in which they were all undertaken.

What is it about home that so lays hold of us, as though it were a planet and we its moon? It brings to mind that line by Edgar Guest: "It takes a heap o' livin' in a house t' make it home." Though it's not necessarily the place you grew up. It could be a country or county or city, or bigger or smaller than any of these. Home is kind of like a favorite pair of jeans that make you feel more you. It seems to contain the ideas of safety and certainty, acceptance, refuge, source. Where you feel most comfortable, perhaps most loved. And your idea of what it is can change, will change, with time. But not entirely. After a long vacation or even a long drive, you long to get back home. Just putting the key into the lock and stepping through the threshold is magic. While living in South Korea, my sister was once part of an exercise where she and a group of colleagues were asked to take a pushpin and stick it into an international map on the wall in the particular place they call home. Having lived in various locations and traveled to somewhere around twenty countries by that time, she was surprised to find this request so challenging, to the point of being overcome by emotion.

Home meant getting back to normal, whatever that is. At the very least, being together again under one roof. Not only feeling more intimately one another's love and care, but even the simplest of things. Coffee tables, shag carpet, knickknacks, portraits, familiar rooms of other than eggshell white. The doorbell and the storm door banging shut. Here and there a skittish cat. Home-cooked meals around a table rather than in bed. Home also meant for Mom and Dad the end of the weekly trips to visit me—which included living out of a suitcase—and for Sarah the end of a single-parent home.

# TOGETHER AGAIN

ONE STRANGE THING about those days is that I hardly remember sharing meals together as a family, just the four of us, or afterwards playing cards or doing other things together. Maybe we did more than I remember, but it's also true that on most weekends and after school was finished there were almost always a couple of my buddies hanging around. I hardly saw Sarah in those days. She was busy being seventeen, and I'm sure the last thing she probably wanted or needed was to spend too much time up close and personal with a situation that would likely fill her mind and heart with more unwelcome questions and ideas.

I don't think any of us expected that being together again would heal everything automatically, but then we hardly knew what to expect of anything. The old family dynamic had been marred beyond recognition, which might tempt you to think it was something we all talked about together, a perfect opportunity for a family huddle, to recalibrate and regroup. But none of us seemed to realize how deeply we had tasted trauma. It was one thing to be adjusting to all that had already transpired, but the ball was still very much in motion. And although our tolerance for trauma had been notched up a good deal, which does make facing future pain that much easier, it also renders you that much more emotionally dull.

It's interesting to think about how each of us distilled it all. Each one so different, each uniquely guided by the host of things we'd lived and learned up to that point. What mattered neither to me nor Sarah probably mattered more than we could guess to Mom and Dad, and vice versa. Like the fact that I was their only son, not to mention their firstborn. The gravest things Sarah and I had faced by then were the deaths of Grandpa and Grandma Boetel and a few classmates. And those things were plenty real and formative on our delicate, developing psyches. But Mom and Dad had been through decades of similar things and more, though no matter what you've weathered, nothing quite prepares you for the thing you could never imagine having to face.

"I don't know how you do it," a friend or two of mine would sometimes say. Incidentally, I didn't either. Had you asked me the day before it happened how I thought I'd handle it, I might have agreed with the friend who one day frankly confessed that, had it been him, he would have promptly driven his chair into the nearest swimming pool. Things weren't peachy, but neither did they seem quite that bleak to me most of the time.

After all, it doesn't take long to settle into new routines that quickly become familiar. Within a few weeks it seems you can actually let your guard down a little without some heartrending emergency pouncing on you out of nowhere. Forgetting what lay behind and thankful to be together again, we each pressed on in our own spheres—Dad and Mom back to work full-time, Sarah with her junior year, and I with further outpatient therapies several mornings a week at the local hospital—each in our own little worlds. To what extent Mom and Dad shared with each other their own inner griefs and fears and questions, or Sarah with them or her friends, I knew not, nor even wondered. I never heard any complaints or heartache from any of them, though I imagine they probably figured I had enough to deal with, so better not to bother me with such. This only makes sense, since a good many of the smiles on my face were to spare them in a similar way. Besides, not to smile and hope for better days wouldn't just make things more unbearable for *them*. For it might be an implicit admission of what one dare not admit, even to himself.

# THIS WAS JUST THE WAY

I'M SO THANKFUL not to have any guilt or regret hanging over my head all these years later. Like anybody, there are plenty of things I could wish I had done differently, but none related to how the injury happened. It simply was what it was. I can't imagine second-guessing that the rest of my life. That must be a horrible way to live. Talk about disability. My family and I were so fortunate. The idea never even surfaced to assign blame. On the one hand, it's a choice you make, but on the other, why we are the way we are and do the things we do goes so far beyond our choices that, at the end of the day, I think it was more of a gift.

Tom and I were just a couple ordinary guys going about our everyday lives when the extraordinary suddenly sprang upon us. I never at any stage wished that I had been on the other end of that transaction. As much as I wished it hadn't happened, it was plain enough to both of us that it could've happened the other way around. From day one there was never even one exchange of heated words or suspicious glances, nor even secret sentiments lurking within, the kind that tend to slip out when you least expect. All of which is to say that there was that much less for all of us to deal with.

We didn't see much of each other in those days. Just like in the hospital, a good number of those who knew me well only rarely, if ever, dropped by. It's not a hard concept to relate to, actually. A number of years ago I consistently avoided a woman at church after her husband died because I didn't know what to say and thought I might stick my foot in my mouth. I thought I might say, "Sorry," but that never seemed right. I felt terrible, but there it was. It never bothered me, though, that some weren't stopping by. Especially Tom. Even then I realized how hard it must have been for him, though he did manage to make it over two or three times. Had our circumstances been reversed, I couldn't imagine driving over to his house and seeing him that way, or trying to make conversation with him and his parents and sister and friends. I was happy enough to have the friends I did coming around, and there were plenty. I don't doubt a few of them might have occasionally eyed Tom with some suspicion, but I never noticed, nor did I ever hear of anyone saying anything to him or behind his back. We were neither drinking nor angry when it happened, and everyone seemed to understand and accept that this was just the way it happened to turn out.

# THE DENNIS BYRD EFFECT

IT WAS ONE of those moments that instantly brings a screaming stadium of fanatics to a deafening silence. The commentators changed their tone as the medical trainers jogged onto the field to surround the motionless body. I don't remember seeing it happen or hearing of it in the news, though back then I didn't watch much news. The man down was defensive lineman and up-and-coming sack leader for the New York Jets, Dennis Byrd, who had intended to sack Kansas City Chiefs' quarterback Dave Krieg. Instead, he collided with teammate Scott Mersereau, ducking his head just before impact. It was November 29, 1992.

A little over a year later, one of my Christmas gifts happened to be his highly publicized and inspirational memoir, *Rise and Walk: the Trial and Triumph of Dennis Byrd*, the dramatic story of his defiance of the odds in refusing to give up as he fought back from paralysis to walk again. The book was followed by a television movie, which aired that February. I'm not sure if I started reading it right away or while at Courage Center, but between that and the movie I was sold. Here was a guy with an injury at the same level as mine, and with a lot of hard work and perseverance he got up and walked again. Little did I realize his injury was much less severe than mine, not to mention the fact that he had the best medical resources NFL money can buy from the moment he hit the turf. But I was nineteen and thrilled that my resolve suddenly had fresh soil in which to push down its eager roots. Dennis Byrd had been paralyzed and walked again, and so would I.

It was the blooming of the same vague notion that had budded back in the hospital, whose fragrance was also savored by family and friends. How the seed first got planted and nourished is a mystery, though it may have sprung up in me spontaneously. And now back on the outside with all things starting to look more hopeful, here was good reason to believe in miracles, as opposed to just hoping into the wind. Here was someone with the same injury, at the same level even, who not only spoke of walking again, but actually did. And everyone believed right along with me. If anyone had reservations that I might be getting my hopes up too high, they didn't say as much.

"Did you see that?" one of my buddies would point out as I lay in bed. "Your big toe just jumped! Try to move it."

Caught up in the moment, I'd give the silent commands and feel—was it feeling?—the given appendage move. Time and again, alone or otherwise, I'd try and try, patiently testing each knee and ankle, finger and wrist, to straighten or bend or lift or twist. And when occasionally something twitched, hope would soar.

# DOWNSTAIRS

My NEW ROOM was upstairs between Mom and Dad's and the bathroom, which had been Sarah's from the time we were small. Back then, mine was the one on the other side of Mom and Dad's, which got converted to a den after I laid claim to the room in the basement in the eighth grade. That basement room had a lake cabin sort of feel, with its cheap wood paneling and even cheaper tan carpet, which had to be replaced one year when I stepped out of bed into more than an inch of water. The room smelled so strongly of mildew in the summertime that it thoroughly permeated the sheets and pillows, and I loved (and still love) that smell and would bury my face in them and inhale deeply. As kids we found it great fun to sleep down there when we had friends overnight. No one remembers when exactly Sarah moved down there—not right away, but sometime before I returned home, the last day of December.

At any rate, it was a blessing just to have a room at home, as opposed to being stuck in a nursing home somewhere. But it also felt like three steps backwards. A far cry from reaching out on my own and laying claim to my own particular place in the world, like all my friends. I could imagine how wonderful that buffer zone of three hours' distance might have felt. But there I was back in the nest as though I had never left. Like a board game where you draw the card that says: *Go Back Ten Spaces,* only it says: *Go Back to Childhood.*

I loved living downstairs. There was nothing not to love about it. The main living space spanned the entire length of the house and was fully furnished with secondhand couches and rocking chairs, TV and stereo, refrigerator, piano, weight bench, and even a pool table. The bedroom was bigger than the one upstairs and had a bathroom attached. In the summer it was five or so degrees cooler than upstairs, and in the winter there was a fireplace. When friends came over it was like you had your own place to yourself. You could crank up the TV and music louder than you could upstairs and talk about whatever you wanted. Even sitting down to do homework in solitude had its own appeal, especially by firelight. It was as good as a kid could possibly expect without rent or utilities. And as the last couple years of high school ran their course, that basement became one of our hotspot hangouts, where we had just enough privacy to get away with more than our share of the usual temptations.

And I'm sure those memories flooded back the first couple times I drove my chair along the edge of the staircase and glanced the long way down, remembering how nimbly I once bound up and down them, grabbing the long black pole at the bottom and swinging my momentum to the right as I let go to stick the landing. The first time the guys carried me down it took four or five of them, grunting every shaky step, as the chair alone weighed nearly three hundred pounds. One evening that summer, in a hurried response to a tornado warning, one beefy buddy, a competitive weightlifter, offered to carry me down over his shoulder. Somewhere in the mix I blacked out, and I remember especially his deep sigh of relief, half-smiling, when I finally came to on the couch.

One thing I couldn't argue with was the timing of my homecoming, as most of my buddies had just finished their first semester of college and had a month off for Christmas break. Sometimes as many as fifteen or twenty a day drifted in and out of the house to keep me company, from late morning until late evening. Many of us had been friends since grade school or shortly thereafter and were like brothers. One after the other they poured forth their soaring highlights, each one trying to outdo the other with tales of classes, dorm life, girls, and newfound pals. All was light and often lewd, and no matter what we did or where we went, we laughed. They were always doing everything they could to include me and help me feel like part of the gang again. Like when Craig bought that pale-yellow seventy-something Caddy, big enough for its own zip code, and they were all so excited to plop me into the front seat and go for a ride.

We were all just a bunch of goofball knuckleheads, in the habit of making light of nearly every situation we encountered. But this crazy thing that had happened to me was such a drastic change, and it really sobered them all a lot. There was plenty of joking and fun, but the amazing thing was that they all went above and beyond in doing everything they could for my family and me. They'd run to the store on errands and carry things into and out of the house at all hours, or help Dad in the yard or me with eating or drinking or in the bathroom. They'd drive me to therapy or anywhere else. A couple alternated lifting me into and out of bed every morning and evening, helped me dress and undress, stretched my arms and legs. God bless you all—you know who you are! And I'd like to think that if it had happened to any of them, I would have been there for them the same way.

In some ways it was nice to get back downstairs now and then for a couple hours and enjoy it for what it was worth. Most evenings we spent upstairs in front of the TV in that crowded little bedroom, the guys lined up in folding chairs on either side of my bed as we guzzled beer and channel surfed. A few times that basement was filled with happy souls, maybe even forty or fifty, everyone loving life and glad to see me back to a semblance of normal with a smile on.

But the days of feeling the pool cue in my hand and strutting around the table talking trash were over. Or feeling the cool, damp tile beneath my stocking feet, or stoking the fire and adding another log, or leaving on a whim and coming in late. Even the way the girls looked at me and talked with me—still friendly and sincere—had changed. The old pecking order no one ever talked about but everyone felt had shifted, without a word or even someone else noticing. Or did they? In any case, the gaps were filled seamlessly without anyone vying for them, as though each one seemed to understand where he fit, like when you remove one marble from a bowl of marbles. There was plenty of laughter and giddy conversation, plenty of watching everyone do the things that I no longer could. Then back upstairs to bed before everyone else—smiles, waves, blown kisses, hugs: "So good to see you, Teddy, sleep well!"

# THE END OF VANITY

TRUTH BE TOLD, I probably spent as much time in front of the mirror in high school as most girls. But getting the bangs to hang down in front just so much, and at just the right angle—even with a cap on—and to stay that way for the next several hours, took some work. While I'm at it I might as well also confess that, yes, this did require a blow dryer, as well as the right mix of gel and hair oil, if you really want to know. I can just see my Dad reading this and shaking his head with his characteristic smirk. Like he does every time he mentions the junior varsity basketball game during which I was benched for having my earrings in (who knew this was a technical foul?). He jokes that he quickly made for the nearest exit.

Things hadn't changed all that much from hospital life, actually, as far as the routines. No more twenty-four-hour staff at your beck and call as often as you pressed your call light, but still sponge baths in bed (for the record, having someone take a warm rag to your face, especially first thing in the morning, seems almost as bad as it did as a kid). A caregiver and nurse from home hospice came out every morning. For some reason (maybe the familiar surroundings?) I noticed more acutely than in the hospital the strangeness of it—grown women doing for me not just what I myself once effortlessly did, but also what my parents did for me back when I was knee-high, which made me feel about that high. But you had no choice. Like it or not, you had to let go and let them. It didn't help matters that sweatpants of various colors composed the totality of my waist-down wardrobe, the logic apparently being that they were easier on the skin than jeans. That had been the protocol in the hospital, so we just stuck to that. To compensate, I did my best to match them with the long-sleeve button-up shirts that were as much a part of my personality as anything. What's more, Mom lifted me into and out of bed when the guys weren't around, which I could hardly believe recently when she reminded me. She also handled my bowel needs in the evenings, which we only did three days a week back then—first in bed, then eventually using what looked like a Vietnam-War-era commode chair, which they strapped me into with one of Dad's old belts.

It was gratifying to do even the smallest of things for yourself. Not only did it feel good, it meant having to rely on others that much less. Brushing my teeth was one of those—since you can about imagine how much fun it is having someone do it for you—which I did with the help of an adaptive splint in the hallway because I couldn't get through the doorways of any of the bathrooms, or under the counters. One evening a week I backed my chair up to a basin full of warm water on the kitchen table and tilted myself back to have Mom wash my hair. She says she distinctly remembers finding sand (presumably from the ball fields) the first time she washed it, though I'm not surprised the bedbound washings at Sioux Valley didn't get it out.

Once summer arrived it felt more normal to see myself in shorts again, with a tan on my legs even. This meant that my catheter tubing and drainage bag—which I wore strapped to one of my legs just below the knee—were out in the open for everyone to see. For some reason this didn't bother me or my friends, though. It was just another part of the new me. Another lovely feature of my wardrobe included a white pair of "compression stockings" identical to pantyhose, ironically called "TED hose," which apparently helped improve circulation. I never quite got used to seeing myself in these and couldn't bring myself to wear them with shorts. On the bright side, I didn't have to put them on myself. Then the emasculation would have been complete.

One of my arms had been in a cast at Sioux Valley to straighten it out because of atrophy, and so for several months I had to wear to bed an arm-length inflatable brace that kept that arm straight. I slept flat on my back every night with two or three layers of blankets pulled up over my head, and often I'd wake in the middle of the night panting and unable to break out of that cocoon, especially with the ever-straight inflate-o-arm. If I needed help, my only choice was to yell. I remember calling out one night over and over, when eventually my sister poked her head through the door, her room being directly below mine. I hated the thought of waking any of them, especially my dear parents, and some nights I'd suck it up and lie there awake for a long time, hoping sooner than later to cool down. But sometimes it felt like I was suffocating, and so, reluctantly, I lifted up my voice. It was selfish, and I realized it, but those were your options.

# SENSE AND NONSENSE

As GOOD AS the company always was, the time always came after each weekend or holiday visit that everyone scattered back to school again and things got suddenly quiet. You could hear the sounds of pans and dishes being put away in the kitchen, or Dad kicking back in his Lazy Boy with the newspaper, the faint noise of television in the background.

I spent the evenings in bed in my room with a TV of my own until lights out, and Mom and Dad would poke their heads in to say I love you and good night. Sometimes one of them would come in and sit next to me, and we'd talk a little. And sometimes, helpless to resist the temptation, I'd crumble and ask why it all had to happen—of all things, why *that*, right *then*, to *me*? And what could they do but gently stroke my forehead and my hair, and silently wipe away my steady tears, and then their own? They did their best to grope for answers, and the one I'd hear the most was the one I probably expected least, which they repeated even when they might have questioned it themselves: "Everything happens for a reason, and God has a purpose in it all." Which I wanted to believe, and tried…and tried…and tried.

I hated to drag them through it with me, but usually it all came gushing up and out like a dry heave, and there was agony in the process but relief in the end. And it really made me wonder if all the things I had gotten away with over the years had finally caught up with me. As though karma might be true after all. Actually, it wasn't karma I dreaded so much as the storyline I had learned just enough about over the years, how the guilty only evade the Just One so long, and then He calls to account. There was more, of course, but that much seemed patently unfair. Not that anyone was claiming to be innocent. But I had to wonder if my crimes were so much worse than those of all my friends. And if that wasn't it, what then? These kind of things just happen—bad things to good people—and sorry about your luck, but you'll just have to make the most of it?

That's when you longed most to reap some vestige of sense from the nonsense, when the God of purpose out of chaos started to speak. I had heard the sermons and memorized the passages—e.g., "Call upon me in the day of trouble, and I will deliver you, and you will glorify me"— and there I was in my own tailor-made situation for cashing in on such claims. Which made it seem the more bizarre that every thirsty breath of prayer rose up into the silence and was gone. Not that I expected anything different. The next time was always the same as the time before.

It wasn't just the darkness or solitude but also the silence that amplified my racing thoughts, when sleep wouldn't come and there was nothing to do but face them. And that's when you found out what all your smiles were really made of. You couldn't even toss and turn, whatever good that might do. There was more presence of mind than in the hospital, more of an alertness to the reality of things. Sometimes the muffled, carefree voices and laughter of friends would drift up from the basement when they were in town, usually still hanging around a while after I was brought up to bed. It sounded like fun down there, the kind I could clearly remember having once upon a time.

Sometimes the Attributes would cross my mind. The savvy-sounding words we'd learned in confirmation class: Omnipotence. Omnipresence. Omniscience. Really? Then He had foreseen. Even had authority and power to intervene, but didn't—or wouldn't. This was perfect purpose on display? Justice? Wisdom? Mercy? Love?

When all else failed, I'd resort to handfuls of carefully thought-through pleas. *Okay, if it has to be this way, could I at least have my arms back? Arms are all I need. I can deal with the rest. Or just my legs. Just something more than this. Please. Is that so much to ask?*

But it was no use. Before I knew it I was waking to another bath in bed.

# ONE DAY AT A TIME

IT'S AMAZING HOW much power some phrases have. Too often we take this totally for granted. Just think how eagerly some people tear into fortune cookies for that little scrap of paper. Or consider how many phrases—good or bad, true or false, like it or not—stick with you to this day, things people have said to you over the years. But I'm thinking of a different kind of power some sayings have. Not power in themselves, like something superstition might tempt you to believe, but in the way that money works—the way you give a dollar in exchange for something else.

*One day at a time* quickly became one of our mainstays. Funny how it seemed to spring into use out of nowhere, almost as if it were not accessible all the time, but only when things get flipped topsy-turvy, cataclysmic. Through all the scrapes and bruises of childhood, I don't remember any of us ever invoking the phrase. Maybe Mom and Dad did, though, in the long weeks after Dad broke his back, when Sarah and I were too young to notice.

I imagine we started using it at Sioux Valley. But by the time I came home we were reaching for it every time we turned around, sometimes several times a day. At least I was, usually at the prompting of Mom or Dad. They were always so faithful to come alongside and repeat the phrase as often as my heart gave way, mostly after the lights went out. Just to make it through another day. That was enough. That was the power of the phrase. And if for whatever reason that wouldn't suffice, you could always fall back on *We'll cross that bridge when we get there*, or *Things could be worse*. There was no need to worry about tomorrow, they'd reiterate, or the week after tomorrow. They would get here soon enough. All you had to do was get through the day. That was the great and simple thing, the most practical advice in all the world. When you couldn't imagine another week of it all, you could always make it through just one more day, which sometimes only meant an hour or less.

*One day at a time* made it possible to finally close your eyes at night and shoo away the demon thoughts that wouldn't leave you be. It made it possible to say you had survived another day. You were the victor and no victim. And it never seemed to wear out, like a no-interest credit card without a spending limit. But more often than not it was you who found yourself weary of the spending spree. Because every day you made it through was always followed by one more. And turning to the phrase again seemed sort of like a child who keeps on tossing into the air a limp balloon.

I don't remember the last time I used the phrase (someone somewhere surely always is); maybe in New Brighton or at Courage. I guess I must have it pretty well.

# BABYSITTER

I HAD A babysitter in the afternoons. Or whatever you call someone who does basically the same thing for a nineteen-year-old.

Most of my weekday mornings were occupied by two or three hours of physical and occupational therapies at the hospital downtown. But with Mom and Dad both working, and once the guys went back to school, it left open the possibility of just me sitting or lying around the house all afternoon, five days a week—which left to guess too many *what if* scenarios, I imagine. I didn't much like the babysitter idea, but I couldn't deny the sense in it.

I could get around most of the upstairs pretty well in my chair, but I couldn't get in and out of the house by myself, if I had to. I couldn't get under the countertops or reach the cupboards. I could open the refrigerator but couldn't get anything out. I could run the TV remote from a book on my lap but couldn't answer the phone. Squeezing both palms together, I could pick up a glass of juice or can of pop and drink it with a straw, though nothing much heavier. I could feed myself with the help of a strap-on splint, but only if there were someone to put food in front of me. And once I was in bed—where I spent most of those afternoons to rest and relieve the pressure on my rear end—my dependence on others was total.

She was a year older than I—my first serious girlfriend, actually. Four months, I think, we lasted, my junior year. Back then, one of the few times Dad got to talk with her, he told me later, *I like her, she's got spunk.* But plenty of time had passed, and so much had changed, and there never really were any serious hard feelings. She, too, had gone to USD but was taking the semester off, pregnant with her first child. I'm not sure how Mom and Dad found out she was available. Probably she had stopped by to visit once or more and the subject naturally came up. It makes me wonder who they might've found if she hadn't been available. Maybe some retired, seventy-something, former battle-axe of a schoolteacher. I shudder to think.

The memories of those afternoons with Dee are very few and fond and come back in sketchy flashes. Mostly I in bed and she close by, with a Scrabble or Parcheesi board between us, daytime talk or game shows on TV. She'd fetch and feed me chips and salsa, homemade ice cream, brownies, pickles, grapes, whatever I wanted. She'd even (cringing at first) put a fat pinch of tobacco in my lip and hold up the spitter for me. She didn't seem like an ex-girlfriend. More like a sister or mother, waddling around with her swollen belly and giving me sass. I remember laughing a lot, and sassing back—our old and easy rapport—and admiring the strangely wonderful symmetry of that belly. And for some reason I still remember the time she tenderly scraped the tan, dried skin from between my fingers with a butter knife.

# GETTING EDUCATED

HAVING PEOPLE VISIT the house was great, but getting back out in the community felt more like living again. And no matter where I went, I got used to being the centerpiece of attention, like a traveling artifact on display. "Freak accident" is how most people referred to what happened. They'd wince as you shared the details, and then invariably you'd hear the phrase, often followed by, "How tragic."

One of the first things you discover is that you've suddenly become everyone's buddy. Just like that. It actually gets to be kind of funny after a while, though a bit disconcerting at first. You're in the grocery store or clinic, and someone passing by suddenly puts their hand on your shoulder. No one ever did it back when you were up where they are, on more equal footing, so to speak, but they don't mean anything by it. They mean well and don't even realize, nor do you for a while, that in a very subtle way they're pulling rank. They're up there and you are down where you are, and for a while it burns you up. *What are they trying to prove?* you wonder. Until you live and learn a little longer, and let it go. But even after you know better you sometimes feel like something less than what you were before, and if you let it take a toll it will. You'll shrink and show your belly like a puppy every time.

"My cousin was a cripple," some guy in his fifties approached me to say one morning on the way into therapy, as though I had some idea of what that had to do with me. Some wink and nod their head with a subtle smile. "Hey, buddy," they say, or "That's quite the chair," or "Better keep it under the speed limit." They're trying, it seems, to bridge the gap between your world and theirs. They're usually strangers or acquaintances. They're not sure what to say, I guess, or maybe they're just sympathetic and want you to feel okay about your situation. Young children stare hard and long, and if they come close enough pepper you with point-blank questions, until cut short by their embarrassed moms or dads, who might or might not jerk them by the arm and apologize with a sheepish smile. Or sometimes the ambitious little helpers get behind your chair and take you for an exciting ride.

You also get the benefit of the doubt more often than not. I'm sometimes shocked how easily even the hardest-looking characters are won over by the quiet demeanor of a broken body rolling by. I remember my caregiver and I being pulled over years ago by the Highway Patrol, and the way the officer's brow lifted ever so slightly as he glanced from my driver back toward me—and then sent us on our way with just a warning. You are also bound to be prayed for sooner or later by some bold soul, more often than not pleading the blood of Jesus over you for your full physical restoration. Beyond that, people are always offering to hold the door for you or give you a push or reach something you can't. Any way you slice it, it's an education you can't put a price on, and one that never ends.

# THINGS YOU WOULD CHANGE

HERE'S ONE I'M tempted to file under: *Things-You-Would-Change-If-You-Could*. But the moment I start thinking along these lines I'm reminded that I need to be careful of saying what ought or ought not to have been. There will always be plenty of circumstances either within or beyond our control that turn out in ways that we later think we'd like to change. And as often as we think we have the answer that would reach the end we have in mind, we ought to ask ourselves what makes us so sure. The very thing we think the remedy may yield an outcome which we might also later wish to change. And besides, just who do we think we are?

I think it goes without saying that relationships are complex. In particular I'm thinking of relationships between siblings, no matter how many there are or what sex they happen to be. In the case of my sister and me, it's just the two of us, and yet even so there are so many dynamics at play that ultimately determine the kind of relationship we have. So many experiences with and without each other have shaped our relationship, for better or worse, some within and some beyond our control. Now and then she'll make a passing comment about me being Mom and Dad's favorite—I can never tell whether or not she's joking, but I always put her off with a laughing "give me a break"—and it's moments like this that make me realize how intricate and fragile these relationships can be.

I really think we fought more often and more fiercely than most brother-sister duos. Mom and Dad had to hire a babysitter the summer after my eighth grade year just to keep peace in the house while they were at work. I was almost fifteen, for goodness' sake! Whether it was our particular temperaments or too much spoiling or TV or sugar that drove us at each other's throats so often, I don't know (though I was the instigator most of the time, I freely admit). It wasn't as though we were raised in a broken home or neighborhood. If anyone had more than their fair share of advantages, we did. But as much as I sometimes hated her, at times nearly to the point of murder (no joke)—for reasons no more substantial than that she might have worn my favorite shirt without asking—we had our lovely moments too.

There are plenty of cheeky photos that tell the tale better than words, but a few memories never captured on camera spring to mind. Leading her by the hand at a daycare we stayed at when we were each a little more or less than five years old. Laughing with her as a teenager in Mom's LeSabre as I drove us to church. Bracing her against me and walking her out of church one Sunday morning after she swooned halfway through the service. Watching her walk down the aisle of the Hitchcock prom and proudly telling my friends that she was by far the prettiest girl there.

My flesh-and-blood kid sis, who has her own story to tell. My brotherly instincts flare up at the least thought of her feelings hurt.

No one meant to ignore her. But you know how it is when you are smack dab in the middle of a situation you don't understand. From the get-go, it happened very casually, at home or around town, among family or friends or strangers—people continually flocking to encircle me like a movie star: "I'll bet you're happy to be home! You look so good! Are you gaining weight? How's therapy? Is there anything you need, dear, anything at all, just say the word." Mom and Dad, too, bent over backwards, day in and day out. And somewhere off to the side was Sarah, for several years, seeing and hearing it all.

Mom and Dad and I were shocked to hear about it— years later. It wasn't even on our radar. Sarah understands now, but it's taken time.

# TELL HER IT'S OVER

I DON'T REMEMBER how it went down, exactly, or when. I know it was a split-second decision made on a whim one afternoon. I'd grown tired of thinking about it—just another inevitable loss, so just get it over with and done. That was my thinking. Why wait?

At first things seemed so hopeful, the prospect of picking up where we had left off. There were excited hugs and long talks on the phone. Eventually a couple evenings together in that little room, I in bed and she in a folding chair squeezed close as possible. But no more picking her up and taking her home. No shower and shave beforehand, deodorant, cologne. No fancy hair or special shirt picked out. No long looks in the full-size mirror. Just soft talking, here and there a kiss, holding hands (rather, my paw-like hand in hers, no fingers interlocked), my parents in the other room. Hardly where we had left off, but you had to start somewhere.

It's amazing what can pass for love when you're young. Not that what you feel isn't real. But love? That's a bit extravagant, like calling abstract scribblings *art*. The trouble is love can mean so many things. At any rate, it didn't take long to recognize what couldn't be ignored, what lingered in the silence of the lulls between the little we had to say— too many changes all at once.

It might've been that I told her best friend to tell her, or else it was one of my friends I told to do it. Whatever the case, the message got through, without discussion or argument. No turning back. That made it easier, but hardly easy. You might compare it to having a very sick pet. You could hang on and watch the poor thing die as nature takes its course, or you could take control and put the thing to rest. It would spare you both worse pain, you thought, and probably it did. On the other hand, I'm sure it was also the same old story of the human heart—always desperate for the upper hand and the final word.

Several months later, at Courage Center, I got to use a laptop computer as "recreational therapy" and wrote her a brief apology (my first and only letter from there, for whatever it's worth). I'd acted like a child and wanted to acknowledge as much. To say that it was nothing personal. There was no malice in it. Disappointment at first, but strangely, and not so strangely, little regret. It was what it was.

# THE PATH TO COURAGE

*THESE MEMORIES ARE filled with holes,* I told myself the other day. That's what happens when you look back twenty years, or even sometimes twenty hours. There's always something missing. But that's all history ever is: Swiss cheese, at best. You don't need every crumb of detail. The holes, I'm sure, are there for reasons we don't need to know. But it puzzled me how I'd arrived at Courage twice. That's how I remembered it, but exactly how I wasn't sure.

None of us is sure how we heard of Courage Center. Dad thinks they told us at Sioux Valley, just before I was discharged. He thinks we must have applied early, mainly because he and Mom had no clue at that point where I would go once they got me home, but also because our first appointment at Courage was in March or April. The reputable Craig Hospital, in Denver, had also been mentioned as an option, though we weren't as thrilled about that because of the distance. Courage was just one state over, in a suburb of Minneapolis. It would still be a five to six-hour drive, one-way, if they ever decided to visit—some of it in dreaded Metro-pace traffic—but that was better than getting on a plane.

I remained as aloof as ever through most of these discussions, though I do remember how bright a hope it seemed. A large facility committed to the express purpose of providing intensive rehabilitation for people like me. I'd be a resident there and probably have a roommate. They'd have on-site caregivers like in the hospital. I'd learn to put on my own clothes, do my own laundry, cook my own meals, and even learn to drive. They'd have all the latest equipment and specialists to help me fight my way to my feet again. Which all sounded too good to be true, but about darn time. I'd be another person altogether by the time they were done with me, back on course to reclaim control of my life.

The problem was we didn't have the resources for it. I'm nearly as clueless now as I was then about all the details. I only knew I might be going and was eager for the opportunity. Apparently it all came down to a call that Dad wound up making to our state senator, Charlie Flowers, who stepped up and made the right calls to the right people in the right places, just in time. It was around five when he called back one afternoon and told Dad that if everything he had told him about my situation was true, then we had a green light to head up there for a mandatory evaluation. As far as I understand, we had no official appointment, and yet for some reason we had to be there by eight the following morning. That meant we'd have to leave by three, and there wouldn't be time to explore how to get me there. It seemed plain that the van that Dad had bought just to get me around town likely wouldn't have survived the Metro pace.

So he called up his old friend Mike, one of the paramedics who had carted me off the ball fields the previous summer, who somehow managed to make available an ambulance. This is just another example of how people went above and beyond on our behalf. In this case it also meant that he and a colleague of his would do the driving, and on top of that wouldn't charge us a penny, because Dad had driven ambulance so many years back.

Of that first trip I only remember them taking me out of the ambulance once we got there, and lifting me from the gurney to my chair. I don't remember the struggle they had getting my mammoth chair into and out of the ambulance or the discomfort I felt in the process after having lain still on my back for so long. Nor do I remember navigating through all those long hallways, nor sitting through multiple evaluations, nor what we had to eat, nor the fact that on the way home we had to detour north around Marshall and continue home through Watertown because of a blizzard, which meant we got home around midnight. "The longest day of my life," Dad added.

# COURAGE CENTER

# ARRIVAL

IT TOOK UNTIL the end of July for an opening to become available. Four or five of my buddies came along with Mom and Dad to help me move things in, though I don't remember Dad with us at all. By then he had bought a slightly better van, and I was much stronger than when we took the first trip, so I was able to stay in my chair and ride up with the guys, while one of them drove my parents in their car.

A skinny man with glasses, spiffy tie, and effeminate voice gave us the official tour. I remember the blood-red tile hallways, the brightness and cleanness of everything, the vaulted ceilings and skylights in places. There was a heated swimming pool behind the glass behind the main front lobby desk. Up and down the elevators, in and out of large white therapy rooms, lots of different exercise machines and cabinets and mats and therapists and assistants (many college-age female assistants). Out back, there was a babbling brook beneath a concrete bridge, arched perfect as a portrait, big enough to hold a dozen wheelchairs at once. Ducks and geese, flowers and foliage, cobblestone-like pathways winding almost all the way around the place. There were meetings and paperwork I don't remember, probably plenty, since I can still see Mom sprawled out on one of the blue-gray sofas just outside one of the second-floor business offices, legs out in front of her, head tilted back, mouth open, as though at home. There was a rectangular room with a long table filled with maybe a dozen or so therapists, and we talked about setting goals and a timetable for leaving. Or maybe that was a few months later.

But the main spectacle was all the wheelchairs. A small civilization of them. You actually had to watch where you were going so you didn't get run over, the manual chairs as much as the electric, though also here and there an unsteady walker, with or without canes. But not so much the old and infirm. Most were under forty, many twenty-somethings. That might've been the most striking thing. Well, almost. Until you passed the woman without arms, well-dressed and walking purposefully, as though the presence or absence of arms was of little consequence. An employee? Or the man in his fifties in plaid flannel shirt and cowboy hat, motionless arms and hands at rest on either side of his chair, a strap across his chest to hold him up. He blew into a straw-like thing to move, and when you looked for legs and didn't see them, you looked away.

It was the kind of place that could shake you if you weren't ready for it. I don't doubt that most visitors kept their tones down, or that young children clung more closely to their parents' sides, though I never noticed. But that's not to say it was a bleak environment, either. There were smiles here and there, everyday conversation, even laughter.

When everything had been taken care of and they had me all settled into my room, Mom lingered, reluctant to leave me alone in a strange place, among strangers. I'll never pretend to understand what mothers feel for their kids, no matter what their age. Even my buddies were half choked up. I imagine I smiled and told them it would be all right. I would be all right.

That evening in the twilight-darkened, mostly empty cafeteria, I don't remember if I sat alone. I remember the largeness and squareness of the room, the blood-redness of the floor, so many round tables without chairs beneath, the sounds of quiet conversation, trays and plates and silverware. And I'm glad my family and my friends didn't stick around to see me there.

# PWD

THAT'S *PEOPLE WITH Disabilities*, to the layman. The demographic I joined without knowing it. The movement with its own history and heroes. The handicapped, disabled, differently able. The special that get their own parking spaces, cut out spots at the movies and stadiums, widened bathroom stalls, the Americans with Disabilities Act. Gradually you learn the lingo and start to speak the language. You find that no one term will work for everyone. It's PC America, after all, and it's not surprising to learn that, like the N-word, some find *gimp* as offensive as others find it funny (hence the bumper sticker of my former downstairs neighbor: *Gimpin' Ain't Easy*). Of course some don't want to be called anything, lest they be pigeonholed by a single term. And what else is new under the sun?

There were gimps at Courage who said it with a smile— my kind of people. It might've been one of them who first called me a quad. I'm pretty sure it was there I first heard the term, though I don't think I referred to myself as one very much, nor have I since. Not that it's offensive or anything. I own it if a situation calls for it. But it's never suited me to make it the centerpiece of my identity, as some do, though it very much is—the fact, not the label.

There were manual chairs and electric chairs; walkers, braces, splints, and canes. Quads and paras, strokes and spina bifidas; cerebral palsies, epilepsies, multiple scleroses; various types of dystrophies, traumatic injuries to brains. Country folks and city folks; different dialects and ethnicities. Mothers, fathers, sons, and daughters—all afflicted, there for help.

I remember seeing for the first time the guys and gals my age in chairs, especially the manual ones, pushing themselves around the campus with a wonderful sort of liberty. There were two girl quads in their early twenties, blonde and brunette, with tan, skinny legs, both alcohol-related accidents. You could imagine them not so long ago walking past a group of guys their age with a self-assured air about them, and heads turning in their direction. Their faces were flint, like wild horses. And man, could they smoke. You never saw a cherry burn so bright.

There was mute young Joe with damaged brain, propelling his wheelchair backwards with one foot, eyes wide mouth open all the time, tobacco spit all drizzled down his beard. Or Jesse, with the pocked and puffy face, nineteen or twenty at the most, a bulky build and stumbly gait—a car or football accident. Or AC/DC T-shirt-wearing Dave, who drooled when he talked and dragged one gimpy leg. One time I saw him hit the floor face first so hard it cracked—the sound, not his face or the floor—and cursing loudly he stood and wiped his mouth. And each new soul you met you wondered who you felt for more, the ones who were or weren't as aware of themselves.

The saddest was the guy next door to us, another one my age or thereabouts. Rumor had it he'd been healthy many years, an otherwise average guy—until one day his movements stumbled. Little by little it all ebbed away, the last bit of strength in his every limb and joint. ALS, Lou Gehrig's disease. I'm not sure I ever met him, only passed him by and tried to smile. He was there when I got there, a blank expression ever so slowly roaming the hallways, his parents and sister sometimes close behind. When he could no longer reach the joystick, they gave him the kind you navigate by leaning your head back into the headrest, and he managed that way for a while. By Christmas he no longer left his room. Rumor had it that his speech had gone. Then he couldn't swallow. Maybe a week or so a later a new quad moved into his room.

But the one that probably surprised me most was the man in his seventies with bone-white hair combed neatly from front to back, whose story I'm not sure I ever heard. A quad with less ability than me, his faithful wife beside him most of the time. It seemed impossible, or maybe just unfair, that such should happen to a man and wife—grandparents, probably—in the sunset of their lives. It taught me that disability doesn't discriminate, if that's the right way to put it (I don't think it is, but it does have a ring to it). It also made me realize more deeply that when one is affected, so are many others.

There was a mix of hope and hopelessness at Courage that can't be put into words. There were those who cared and those who couldn't have cared less, and you all rubbed shoulders sooner or later. The first few days there were a little like the first day back at school as a kid. Silent, guarded eyes marked you everywhere you went, made you feel the stranger you were, though you usually weren't the only new arrival. At any rate, sooner than later they were asking you what happened, and you'd explain and then ask them the same. Some didn't have much to say about it. *It happened, so what. Life sucks.* But others you didn't even have to ask. You only had to hesitate midsentence and they were off down memory lane, regurgitating highlights of a time when life was so much different. They'd carry you along with them as long as you would listen, caught up in their own momentum, gesturing as best they could to keep up. They'd driven the fastest, dated the prettiest, and done the craziest things no one else would do. If you got a word in edgewise, you probably threw in your own two cents of some of the same. Until eventually the stories trailed off into silence, and you were left there looking at one another, and the subject quickly changed to something else.

# THE EYES HAVE IT

I THINK IT was the eyes that tipped you off. They say so much. I heard recently that fifty-five percent of our communication is body language, if that means anything. At any rate, there were the two groups, with different kinds of eyes.

I imagine at first it seemed like we were all more or less in the same boat, each one with his and her unique affliction. And of course we were. But soon enough the distinctions became plain, the main ones anyway, and you fell in with whom you fell in. There were those of us in chairs and those who were not, and the chairs would often hang together, especially the manual ones. Which I suppose is only natural. It helped to see and talk with other quads, how like and unlike you they were, how they did the same things you did, a little differently. And not just the quads. You learned from everyone and came to see how fortunate you were. But the difference in the eyes meant more than anything, I think, in steering you toward the ones you clicked with most.

And this matter of the eyes seemed somehow linked to whether or not you'd been afflicted all your life. For the one group, it was a genetic defect or other complication during pregnancy or childbirth, and they were affected from the get-go, or not so long thereafter. Sometimes it touched the mind to various degrees. Most used electric chairs, though a few were in manuals or managed to hobble around with braces or canes. I'd seen the likes of them somewhere before, the tender eyes and fragile posture, so familiar. Where was it? The old hallways and lunchrooms of yesteryears, that's where. The relegated ones the rest of us avoided, who had their own special department and teachers, their own lunch table, their own pre-appointed social destiny, by and large. At whom I hate to admit I far too often laughed with friends.

They weren't your friends. They were too unlike you, and separated from you anyhow. While you were busy playing sports, out on dates, coming and going as you wished, what was it they were busy doing? Not habitually staying out until the wee hours of the morning, probably, nor falling prey to peer pressure in all the usual ways. Even if you had thought to try to bridge the gulf between your life and theirs, what would your friends have said? And here they were again, different faces home to different souls, a little older but much the same. Yet strangely there was still this separation. Not that you weren't friendly when you shared with them an elevator or table in the cafeteria. After all, you finally shared some common ground—but not enough, apparently. Intensity, upheaval, listlessness—were not the things their eyes contained. Just mostly resignation, introversion, isolation—to which you were not drawn.

I know it's dangerous talking this way. It doesn't mean there aren't exceptions. There are plenty. I have several friends who are, who would quickly take exception to the notion all alike grow up this way—pampered, sheltered, far too much, which only further impairs. At any rate, their childhoods were nothing like mine, or any of my friends'. I'm certain I can say that much. I'd never been the odd man out, nor known how it feels to have your classmates staring all the time, holding you at arm's length. My buddy Troy— cerebral palsy from the womb—once told me how the kids would knock his canes out of his hands on the way to class, then toss them far enough away that he'd have to crawl to get them back. I've got nothing to compare with that.

And then there was the other group, whose eyes held more. Something clearly different. What was it? Something of a piercing quality. A knowing or wounding, of sorts. Very subtle. Maybe like the difference in a wolf, once he's tasted blood. You recognized it right away. They hadn't been sheltered, that's for sure. They had grown up much like I had, free to run and swim and ride a bike and do ten thousand other things they probably took mostly for granted. Until it happened—most often suddenly, and after that they were never the same. They had been used to the one perspective always, and then that point of view changed drastically. An opportunity of sorts arrived, though most would not have called it that—the chance to see the world through different eyes. This is why theirs often proved the steeper loss. Because you don't know what you've got until it's gone, right? And so much had gone.

It surprised me how so many in the other group didn't seem too bothered by all they'd never done. *The things they'd missed out on* is the way I would have thought of it. They'd never known what any of it was like. On the other hand, that meant there was nothing for them to miss, and you had to envy them for that. I'm glad I got the chance to do it all, short-lived as it turned out. At any rate, I sometimes wonder how much different things might be if I had never left that room at Mom and Dad's.

# IN ONE SENSE

DESPITE ITS DOWNSIDES, there's something to be said for this experience of disability. I mean after having lived one way for so many years, one lifestyle from a particular perspective, and then just like that you find yourself taking things in from an altogether different vantage point. Regardless of the overall quality of the new perspective, there is the unvarnished contrast and all it has to teach. For whatever it's worth. And few get the chance.

It's an experience that sometimes reminds me of the return of King Odysseus to Ithaca after having been gone so long and thought dead. Disguised as a lowly beggar passing through his overturned kingdom, he finds himself treated much differently by many of his subjects. Or imagine going to bed white and waking up black, or vice versa. Instantly you start to notice things you didn't before. And even when you don't, someone in the same boat as you helps you out.

Like the afternoon my roommate, an African-American, let me in on the fact that I had joined the ranks of the minority, which apparently hadn't dawned on me. He wasn't out to teach a lesson, just making a passing comment that he was a *double minority*. That set me to thinking, as did a lot of things he said. He was always dropping catchy adages here and there, which had a sort of grandmotherly wisdom about them: "Disability is ninety percent mental, ten percent physical," "An ounce of prevention is worth a pound of cure," "Disability is a heartbeat away." I think he probably thought I was about as country as they come, and probably I was, and maybe I still am. And whether in spite of or because of that, or both, he took me in like a kid brother.

As for his story, he was walking across the street one day in broad daylight when out of nowhere came a drunk driver doing sixty miles an hour. He was thrown into the air and came down directly on top of his head, though by some miracle he escaped brain injury. He was between forty and forty-five but could have easily passed for thirty, I thought, another incomplete C5-6 quad whose strength and dexterity discouraged me at first. To look at his bulging arms and shoulders, you wondered if he had *any* limitations. The incompletes pushed faster, transferred themselves into and out of their chairs and beds, even showered and dressed and undressed themselves and more, though sometimes needing help with one thing or other. One image that sticks with me is occasionally coming back to the room to find him staring intensely into his full-length mirror, repeatedly pumping heavy strap-on weights above his head, his boom box blasting with Keith Sweat.

And yet he was only human, and now and then something went wrong with his catheter or bowels and he'd wind up soaking wet or worse, and his normally playful mood would suddenly turn. You'd hear him hollering from down the hallway, every expletive and epithet imaginable, and you kept your distance as long as you could manage, and if you happened to be in bed you either looked the other way or pretended to be asleep. You felt for the caregivers trying their best to help him get cleaned up as he gnawed their hides, always their fault, something not tied the right way or this or that was far too something or other. And when his wrath eventually subsided there was silence in the room for a long while. And you left him to himself and didn't say a peep until he spoke up first, and not long after you were joking like there never was anything wrong.

But back to where I started. This has nothing to do with whether you wished things were otherwise. You may say you would rather not have had the opportunity of the new perspective. That's fine. You are entitled to that. This is only food for thought.

# POKER NIGHT

I'M NOT SURE what else I did with my evenings for nine months. There were board games, but no one ever seemed interested. Actually, I wasn't even that interested, maybe at least partly because so many things required a fair amount of dexterity, otherwise you needed help, and that has a way of dampening your enthusiasm. Some went to the bars on weekends, or as a group to the Chanhassen Dinner Theatres. But neither appealed to me for some reason. I remember leaving once each for a haircut, a church service, and a group Christmas shopping adventure (picture an old school bus with most of the seats removed and packed with over a dozen wheelchairs). Otherwise, it was poker or watching TV in bed.

It seems like there was a regular poker night, singular, though maybe they played throughout the week. Just down the hall from us in the fluorescent-lighted kitchenette, the big-round table nearest our room. It cost you a dollar per hand, and there was no upping the ante or anything like that. The cards got dealt and you had one chance to throw what you didn't want. You either lost your dollar or won the whole pot. I don't think I played more than once a week or let myself spend more than five bucks a night. I remember winning, though, and the thrill of it, which was different when you were playing for piles of cash. Different, I mean, than playing for chocolates or quarters when you were a kid. This also meant you felt your losses more keenly too.

There were usually five or six guys, never gals, most in manual chairs, though there were a couple lower-functioning guys like me. There was one quad with a brain injury who, when he played, would often forget what hand beat what, and someone would have to remind him, and he'd say, "Oh, yeah, right," and then ask again five minutes later. Some who couldn't hold their cards used plastic or wooden racks with a series of slits that held them. I liked mine face down in front of me on the table like a couple other guys did, which was tricky because you had to lift them just enough to see them but not so much that you exposed yourself. One by one you peeked and at the same time tried to remember what each one was, and sometimes you had to look again. And again.

And it wasn't unusual for something so simple to remind you of home and the good old times—when you didn't have to remember your cards. You held them right out in front of you like everyone else and thought nothing of the feel of them in your hands or how so casually you switched them around and grouped them by color or number or suit, spacing them ever so evenly as though it made some difference. Which also might have brought to mind the many times at home or at the farm with the aunts and uncles, cousins, Grandpa and Grandma gathered now and then at Christmas time or for a wedding or funeral. And out would come thick decks of cards and off went the tablecloth in the dining room ("We want to hear the sounds," I heard my cousin Megan recently say as she stripped it off). For the oldies, it was always pinochle or five hundred, hours of it, which they'd grown up watching their parents play with the neighbors, all farm families. "We were too poor to do anything else," I've heard them so often say. You could remember as a kid sitting around asking how to play, and without looking up from their cards they would murmur things like "meld" and "double run," and sooner or later "just watch," which you tried your best to do but never could, probably because you could only stand to sit still there five minutes at a time. And there was the way soft-spoken Grandpa Boetel would sometimes slam his fist down on the table without a trace of anger, and his card would slide right to the center, and how Aunt Marie called Grandma "Toots" (pronounced *boots*). They'd play husbands versus wives, or other pairings of in-laws, and every now and then amid the sound of shuffled cards and the occasional snide comment, you'd hear them all erupt with shrieks of victory and dismay, always laughter and a recap of who bid what and who got set how much, and if Grandma was on the losing side and Grandpa laughed, she'd slug him in the arm.

But you didn't want to linger there too long. Because there was no going back—not in any of the ways you wanted to.

# RANDOM FIRST TIMES

THAT HAIRCUT WAS my first time alone out in the big city, unless the church service was. In both cases the memories are little more than vapors. But I do remember that the bus brought me right to the front door of some random place I suppose I somehow found (before the Internet, fancy that) in the colossal Twin Cities Yellow Pages. An old-fashioned kind of place with all-male barbers and the classic red-white-and-blue swirly barber pole outside. For whatever reason, I had borrowed Eddie's manual chair, which had no wheelie bars in back and no seatbelt. This meant that before we even left the Courage parking lot, the driver having raised me up on the lift and given me a gentle shove to help me get over the subtle bump between me and the inside of the bus, the chair and I spilled ever so gracefully backwards, my head-neck-and-shoulders eventually meeting first the opposite wall and then the floor—my first, though not my last, time tipping in a manual chair. I didn't come out of the chair, fortunately, which was amazing, given the awkward angle and considerable momentum. But it was even more amazing that the driver somehow managed by himself to get me back upright again.

It was also at Courage that I had my first shower in over a year. Since the evening before that morning I'd been carted off the ball fields. After a year of bed-bound sponge baths, you can about imagine how refreshing that felt. Actually, no, you can't. Don't even try. At any rate, I had gone from *taking* showers to *receiving* them, although in one sense showering is as much a passive as active experience. There is something so intimate about a shower. It is a kind of sanctuary, your own personal space and time alone to yourself, the healing sound of water continually cascading over your multiplied features and pitter-pattering down to the floor. Some of my best ideas come in the shower. But back then it was all new, and it was suddenly you and someone else in there—you in your birthday suit and they all covered and composed—and that took some getting used to. Especially when it was a gal your age or thereabouts, and during her orientation you had a nurse in there with you, too, interspersing her how-to demonstration with a-little-too-specific descriptions of certain parts of your anatomy (using textbook terms never helps matters). Not that putting a guy in there with you sweetened the deal any, which happened just as often. Sometimes it reminded you of showering for the first time with a locker room full of your sixth-grade gym classmates, though in that case you were all in the same uneasy boat. Needless to say, I had never imagined what a priceless commodity privacy had been.

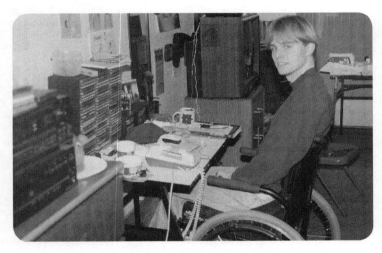

Our room at Courage Center, 1994

# WHAT I HAD

I HAD A room at the end of the hall with a patio view (second room from the end, to be exact). I had the half beside the bathroom, closest the door, and half a closet, too, with sliding doors, a curtain between our beds to pull whenever the need arose. I had a little white desk, a tacky chest of drawers; CDs and stereo, books and picture frames; a thirteen-inch TV with VCR; a phone that called long-distance every week. I had a commode chair with a hole in the seat and a bucket below, which you could hear rattling all the way down the hallway each morning as someone pushed it toward our room. I had a bright red Marlboro cap a friend back home gave me before I left. I had a mop of bleached-orange hair with dark brown roots, and hands that worked like oven mitts. I had shriveled legs that bounced around each time I pushed over the smallest crack, and I had to stop and wait for them as spasms shot up my back.

I had more bad habits than good. I had too many memories. I had a problem reconciling present things with past. I had a streak of wanting to believe I was okay with the way things were. I had a will to wish for better things. I had plans for if I someday walked again—many plans. I had a tendency to lie awake at night and try to put to rhyme and rhythm all I felt deep down, adding stanzas night by night and hoping to remember the following day (example: On one cold and rainy day/A kid got hurt in town/He couldn't move his arms or legs/Or sit up on his own). I had a small devotional Mom would send me every couple months—*Our Daily Bread*—and sometimes it gave nourishment, though usually little more than crumbs.

# NOTHING TO LOSE

IT STARTED THAT first week. Maybe even that first afternoon after my folks and friends left. I'd just come back to the room, and Eddie was out on the balcony.

"You wanna hit this?" he asked as I pulled out there and caught an unmistakable whiff of what he meant. I'd never tried it, except once earlier that summer back home, late one night in bed (we nearly burned a hole in the air mattress on which I lay)—but it didn't take. Some of my buddies had started our senior year, but I always refused, fearing addiction. I guess the *Just Say No* campaign must have worked on me, though for some reason I never feared drink the same way (maybe because there was always some around the house). Even with my daily chewing habit, which started in eighth grade, I would periodically quit for a week or two just to make sure I wasn't hooked. An addict was something I knew I never wanted to be. It seemed like a weakness and a real danger. But out on that balcony I figured I had nothing to lose, which is probably the same reason I started smoking not so long thereafter.

There was no reason not to. Death no longer seemed the fearful enemy it once had. On the contrary, it held out a tempting promise: it could all be over with sooner than later. And sure enough it wasn't long before you discovered who did and who didn't, and you gathered in one room or other, usually ours. Sometimes a line or circle of four or more chairs squeezed as close as possible, and those who could would pass the little smoking scrap or pipe to the next in line, or hold it for the ones like me who couldn't. When it was nice out, we were on the balcony, and in the colder months right there in the room in front of a football or basketball game, a smog-like haze hanging over our heads. I was always astounded that we never got caught, even when one afternoon a couple of the higher-ups from administration happened to knock on the door and pop in, for what reason I don't remember. And what started as once or twice a week soon became daily, twice-daily, more than twice-daily. Though every now and then I'd still stop for a week or two, just to make sure I wasn't in over my head.

# DEATH OF AN IDEA

I couldn't say when I gave up on the idea of walking again. Probably not long after leaving Courage, if not before. It wasn't any one experience in particular that did it, or something that someone said. It took a while and was sort of a gradual letting go—or maybe wearing down is a better way to put it. The way a sheet of ice, after so long, eventually gives way from the side of a glacier—the point at which resolve dissolves.

I was so determined for so long and believed with all my heart I could do it. My identity and future were all wrapped up in it. If I could just keep thinking positively and pushing myself, eventually I'd overcome. I'd defy the odds like others had. That was the general mantra. I'm not sure I had any other expectations, nor did I have a contingency plan in the event things didn't work out. I can still picture Eddie and I and one other quad with weights strapped to our arms some evenings as we pushed circles round and round the lonesome square of hallways that enclosed the first-floor kitchenette. The same look on our faces. Not looking for applause, just hungry. Though I'm not exactly sure what they were after. As for me, I knew what I wanted. But there came a point somewhere when the cat was out of the bag, and there was no getting him back in.

# HAMA DAYS

# RIPE FOR CHANGE

I INVITED MY old buddy Jason to come room with me. The one who probably helped me more than any other friend back home when I first returned from the hospital. As far as I remember he was on academic probation (too much fun his freshman year) and was living with his mom and stepdad near Fargo, working the night shift of an assembly line job. I said it was a two-bedroom place and there wouldn't be any rent if he did some of my cares. Did he say yes right there on the spot? Maybe I told him to think it over and let me know.

What a couple of greenhorns we were, both so ripe for change. When I think of those days all I can do is shake my head in wonder. We moved in sometime in March, a brand-new apartment complex in New Brighton, a cheery suburb northeast of Minneapolis. I had applied to five or six places throughout the Metro as part of my "transition therapy" shortly before leaving Courage and somehow wound up hitting the jackpot. I even had my choice of apartments. It just so happened they were specifically designed for people in chairs, which meant automatic lobby doors, counters and appliances you could roll under, showers into which you could roll. It was as accessible as Courage and as elegant as an upscale hotel.

I'd already met with the public health nurse before leaving Courage and was granted from the state about eight hours of care per day, which I split into four shifts. Since we were together most of the time, Jason took most of them, except the ones involving bowel care. So by and large it was just the two of us together all day most days, which didn't feel like a working relationship. It felt a little like old times, in fact, as we were old pals, almost from elementary school. And that made it nice, more of an even playing field, rather than employee-client. It was an arrangement we both loved. Other than me he really didn't have a boss to please, and there was no worry of his being late or of having to commute anywhere.

We had no schedule, nothing we really had to do most days. Our schedules more or less revolved around each other, so we pretty much did whatever we wanted at any given moment. It allowed me the luxury of not having to have my day broken up by other caregivers coming in every several hours. I must have been getting Social Security by then because there was usually money in the bank. And man, did we blow through money. After all, there were so many blank walls and shelves, empty drawers and cupboards that needed filling this minute with pictures and knickknacks and kitchenware of every kind. So off we'd go in the van—*Baby Brown*, we called it—bound for one of the malls or grocery stores. That was the most regular thing about our lifestyle: our perpetual, haphazard busyness with one undertaking or another. Every afternoon had its adventures. Taking my chair up and down the escalators at the mall is one image that comes to mind. All we needed was an idea to pop into one of our heads and that became our pet project for the day.

I'd gone from waking every weekday at six in the morning in a setting where your schedule and accountability were taken seriously to one where neither order nor accountability really existed, unless you cared enough to see to it yourself. There were no more therapists to challenge and guide your motivation. No more *supposed to do* this or that in a certain timeframe. No setting goals or progress monitored, nothing written down and measured week by week. Probably we had both had enough of *must* and *need to* for a while and were perfectly content to let them go.

On the other hand, it was a contrast I'm not sure I noticed much—for a while. I had grown quite used to having decisions made for me—having staff hired and trained and at my beck and call most any time, without my ever needing to pay too much attention, just say the word or pull the cord and there they were to help you out. So I imagine I took for granted that the transition would be seamless and wouldn't require too much effort. But it did take effort, as my "transition therapy" at Courage made clear my last couple months there. Before even one caregiver or nurse stepped foot inside my door I would first need to make calls and appointments, evaluate who would and wouldn't be suitable, and who would get to work how much, and on which days. It was a big and sudden jump from being managed to self-management.

I met my first caregiver while still at Courage, a thin, quiet man in his late thirties to mid-forties. By the time we were in the apartment, the national news was full of talk and stenciled police sketches of someone they were calling the "Unibomber," and we half-joked that maybe this was the guy. He might have worked one or two shifts, and after that we never saw him again. Then there was the stripper, about our age, who almost dropped me one morning as she transferred me to the shower chair. Every now and then I see her last name on the side of a semi-trailer and remember those days. She didn't last more than a week either. That's how it was. You met them, and if they seemed semi-normal they were soon on the schedule, and if, for whatever reason, they didn't show up one morning, you'd have to give a yell and wake your sleeping roommate. But fortunately that just happened once or twice.

# MORE OF THE SAME

MOST EVENINGS WE sat around channel surfing or watching movies, usually just the two of us. It didn't take long to meet the neighbors, two of them quads who had also been recently discharged from Courage, both before I arrived. The one at the opposite end of the hall was another C5-6 incomplete who sold ganja and told us from the first evening he met us that if we ever needed any we knew where to find him. And find him we did.

Before long we were having people over nearly every weekend for pizza and poker and party. Playing cards got old fast, but it was something to do, and it was always more interesting having people over. There were actually several people from Courage who lived in the building, most of which we never hung out with, except on nights like that. Sometimes there were eight or ten people at the table, even the caretakers of the building, a husband and wife in their early to mid-fifties. At the least it broke up our routine and was another opportunity to leave the confines of reality for a few short hours, though of course you never thought of it in those terms.

Everything was upside for the first several months or so. Isn't that how it always is? We had our daytime routines and our evening routines. The weekdays were no different than weekends, except that if we wanted the hard liquor on Sunday we had to cross the border to Wisconsin, which I remember doing on at least one occasion. I got used to chasing my meds with beer or shots or stinking smoke, all three some evenings. There was no fear in any of it. No real thought of "What if something serious happens?" I wondered sometimes what I'd do if someone offered us some other drug, maybe a hallucinogen. I wasn't so sure that I'd refuse. It just didn't matter. The basic rationale was, "If something happens, you've got to go some way, why not this way?" It wasn't like the future was holding out all sorts of tantalizing prospects to choose from. I'm not sure what either of us looked forward to in those days. I did my best not to look too far forward. In any case, if anyone else felt the way I did, no one was saying anything. But I do remember thinking one evening—after hearing someone say for the umpteenth time, "I could drink you under the table any day!"—*is this really all I have to look forward to for the next how-many years?*

# BLITZKRIEG

THAT FALL I enrolled in a couple of introductory English classes at a community college half an hour from our place. It broke up our mundane schedule a little and offered a refreshing change of direction and purpose. The first class bored me silly and might have been part of the reason I started showing up high (actually, by that time we were going everywhere high, which I was in the habit of justifying because it also temporarily relieved the muscle spasms in my back and legs). The second class was much more challenging and engaging. I wrote essays on the importance of music, the difference between daytime and evening commercials, the pros and cons of living in an off-campus apartment in getting a college education. I sat at the back table by the entrance with three or four others who looked like they might be high-schoolers, one of whom took notes for me. And in the end I somehow finished with an A.

Anyway, one afternoon in that second class, either while the teacher was lecturing or maybe as we were all working quietly on our next assignment, I felt a funny chill race down my spine. Not like a shiver or goose bumps; neither ordinary nor unfamiliar. More of a prolonged tingle that starts at the base of the brain and grips you instantly, probes deeply and lingers, even pulsates like a heartbeat, an oddly satisfying sensation, a kind of numbness in the back of your head and neck. And with it, somewhere down in the innards, an all but silent churning stirs. I knew instantly and hoped against hope. That is, I knew something was amiss, just not exactly what. Sometimes it's the bladder, sometimes the skin breaking down somewhere, or sometimes, as in this case, the worst-case scenario. Each feeling has its own telltale subtleties that it sometimes takes years through trial and error to distinguish. And at that stage it was all Greek to me.

Although some subtle gurgling sounds continued, no one at my table seemed to notice. Or had they? What were those casual sideways glances? I tried as nonchalantly as possible to take a few subtle sniffs, which only confirmed my fears. Sneaking nervous peeks at my crotch, I could see the material puffed up ever so slightly, and when I pressed a couple knuckles against it, it squished around like pudding. I don't remember if that was the first time or not. I don't remember another episode like it, but it seems like it happened more than once around that time. It had happened to Eddie a couple times back at Courage, which he called *invols* (i.e., involuntaries)—actually, *f—ing invols* is what he called them. One of my current caregivers calls them *blitzkriegs*, after the German military tactic during World War II that combined speed, surprise, and power.

It was a warm and sunny autumn afternoon, and getting out into the fresh air after class at least brought peace of mind that no one could smell you out there, unless they were downwind. Jason pulled up sometime later, not in the van as usual but in an unfamiliar, shiny silver Chevy Cavalier. He'd been talking about buying it, and there he was, all excited and proud to have a nice car to call his own for the first time in his life. And what's more, he thought he'd share his joy by giving his good buddy a chance to ride up front like old times. I'm glad I don't remember what happened to the expression on his face when I broke the news. It was rush hour, so going back to fetch the van wasn't an option, though he did happen to have a small hand towel that he laid on the seat before lifting me in. And though that didn't completely protect his brand-new passenger seat, it could've been worse. On the other hand, the start and stop traffic of that forty-five minutes or so never seemed to take so long.

Once home, it was back to bed and right into the shower. Though not so lickety-split. Nothing is ever so simple anymore. To begin with, you simply cannot imagine the sour-smelling, gut-wrenching stench from which you instinctively turned your face the instant it hit you. After all, I'd been stewing in it for over two hours. There was no easy way about anything. Even from that first button and zipper, it was everywhere, even somehow on my shirt, spilling out almost like vomit; a sickly, yellowish muck. My favorite light-beige khakis from the Gap were history, straight into the trash, along with my boxers, shirt, and socks. It was a miracle if any square inch of my hairy legs escaped untouched, though I'm not sure any did. Then, trying his best to lift me without soiling himself, my buddy put me in the shower chair and rolled me naked through the bright mid-afternoon living room and into the stall, where the only thing to do was hose me down from a few feet away, like an animal at the zoo, the warm water and steam only exacerbating the smell.

I remember wondering if there were any two human beings anywhere else on earth spending an afternoon in such a way. It was a terribly depressing scene, and as bad as I felt myself, I felt even worse for my friend. It was the very last thing you wanted to have to ask anyone to help you with, let alone your old pal. It was not the kind of work he had signed up for, and it was new territory for both of us. It wasn't like I knew how to coach him through it, if even that would have helped. It was one thing to have someone showering and cleaning, toileting and dressing you every day in what was starting to feel like life as usual. But it was another thing altogether to lie there like an infant all messy and vulnerable and not be able to help or change matters the least little bit. All you could do was lie there and stare at the ceiling, grasping for some silver lining.

I wondered how many more times I could possibly stand to live through such. I wondered if it was things like that that drove people insane after so long. I wondered if there was a woman on planet earth who could possibly consider living with me as wife for the long haul—after all, such a catastrophe might happen any time, maybe even on our honeymoon. But more than anything I wondered what our college buddies were doing at just that hour, the middle of an otherwise ordinary afternoon. Maybe they were getting out of classes or playing hacky sack or on their way to work or meeting a new girl for the first time, maybe even a future spouse. One thing was certain—they were not doing what we were. Maybe they couldn't even have conceived that anyone would ever have to spend an afternoon in such a way.

The next day we went to Pawn America and I bought my buddy a few CDs. He'd been paid for that long hour or so, but that hardly seemed adequate. I felt terrible and thought a few CDs were the least I could offer.

# HAMA DAYS

IT WAS LATE one night and we were parked in front of the
TV, most likely watching MTV. High as kites, probably.
The music video of a popular song was just beginning or
ending, and the tiny white letters appeared on screen with
the name of the artist and title.

"What was the name of that?" I asked. "Hama?"

"What?" said my friend, maybe with a smirk. "Hama?"

Then he broke out laughing and asked what possibly
made me think it could be called that, of all things? *Hama?*
It wasn't even a word. Didn't I know that? But never mind.
It was late and dark, and I was in a fog and needed glasses
besides, and it was a single word with four letters, and I had at
least got that much right, hadn't I? Not that any of that makes
up for it. It was called *Name*, and I'd heard it many times and
should've known. It's a moment that's become something of
a symbol of those days, the very apex of nonsense. And as
you might imagine, I never heard the end of it.

# WHAT IT MEANT

JASON MOVED OUT sometime in December. He wanted to give college another shot. I don't remember if it struck me as good news or bad. It caught me off guard. I recall feeling anxious, the way I think we often feel whenever things change for us in ways we didn't expect or choose for ourselves. But I was happy for him too. He was as ready as I for another change. It was forward progress.

That meant, for starters, his shifts would need to be covered. I wasn't losing a friend, but I was losing a roommate and employee. It meant that I'd be on my own in ways I hadn't been before. If someone didn't show up in the morning, I'd be in bed until the noon shift. It also meant that it would be just me and someone I hardly knew alone in the apartment several times a day, particularly when I was next to helpless in bed. But I was fortunate. I had one guy who had worked for me at Courage who not only cared and picked up a number of the open hours, but he also became a good friend. There was a retired guy from New York who had a full-fledged accent and wore a dash of ash on his forehead during Lent. A couple of young ladies in their twenties who had also worked for me at Courage, beautiful but spoken for, who had no problem lifting me. And a lifetime bachelor in his fifties who started talking to me from the moment he arrived at six a.m., cracking open a can of soda and nonchalantly yanking up the blinds. So as far as help goes, the transition was pretty smooth.

It also meant I had a lot more time on my hands, much of which was time alone. I noticed the silence for the first time in a long time, my first real taste of being on my own. It reminded me of the times when Jason would run to the store on an errand for an hour or two and leave me to myself, and I savored the privacy as long as it lasted, as I'm sure he also did. But after a couple weeks without him I felt like I had lost a spouse. Even if he was somewhere in the building or in his bedroom, there was comfort in knowing there was someone else not far off, both for company and a sense of security. But from that point on it would be just me and the silence.

It also meant the weekend party patterns faded, like storm clouds broken up by a change in the landscape. And though that proved to be a welcome change, the neighbor down the hall and I would still get together a couple times a week and smoke up and play cribbage and listen to music or watch a movie. Sometimes he'd cook supper for us, and because he had a lot more strength and dexterity than I did, he did most of the work, though I did help set the table. "Two quads can make it together in this world," he liked to say with a proud smile. He didn't seem to want much more than some of those routine leisures, though every now and then he'd carry on a little about his dream of one day owning his own bar, *The Rusty Cage*.

Because of the cold weather and snow I took the winter semester off school. Most days I spent in front of the computer, playing solitaire, poker, golf, or pinball, sometimes wasting entire mornings and afternoons. It felt like a pretty wasted existence to fritter away so many hours that way, and yet in another sense it didn't matter. It passed the time. But of course you can only take so much of anything, and before long I moved on to novels—Dean Koontz and Stephen King, mostly—I who hadn't read much of anything growing up, aside from a few Hardy Boys adventures, and *Robinson Crusoe* and *The Karate Kid*. But to my surprise I found myself really digging in and enjoying it. Stranger still, I began to have the nerve to think that I could write the stuff myself, and soon I began spending most days playing with verse and meter and short fiction, which was even more gratifying than the reading. But it's also true that as those winter days slowly ambled by, that's about all I was feeling gratified about.

# A SIMPLE PLEA

I CAN'T SAY when it was. But it was sometime after the blitzkrieg episode(s), and after Jason left. I think it was a month or week before the invitation came that proved to be the answer in disguise. But I can't forget it, blurry as the scanty details are—in bed like so many other nights, the lights off, by myself.

Moments like that are so few and far between. It's not every day we reach a crisis. We keep ourselves so busy. We do everything we can to avoid these moments. They hurt and often leave scars, and how content we are to let ourselves believe what we might find we don't in fact believe if but for just a few short minutes we thought things through, really got to the heart of matters. But we don't like that. It makes us squirm. "It'll be okay," we tell ourselves. "Just keep plugging away."

I always took for granted there must be a God up there who is so much bigger and fuller and different from us. I'd prayed to Him since I was a kid. I never thought too much about what if He wasn't up there after all. I didn't even notice in that moment that although I talked with Him as though He was, my heart was not so sure. Is that not strange? To try to speak to one who you don't know for sure is really there?

It might have been the most visceral utterance I ever breathed. Something along the lines of: "If You are up there, I need to know. I'm tired of this. I can't do it anymore. If You're real, show me."

# AN INVITATION

HE HAD VISITED me once or twice while at Courage Center. He was the pastor of a small church in New Hope, the cousin of the father of my buddy Tom from the ball fields. His cousin had mentioned to him that I was at Courage and that I might benefit from a visit from him. The only thing I remember of one of those visits is a brief conversation we had about God. The exact words elude me, but the gist was that he offered something I refused. "I'm not ready for that," I think I said. I think I said I believed in God and was content where I was at.

And then many months later, he dropped by the apartment a couple times. I remember him taking me out to eat at least twice: once, I think, while Jason was still there (we went to TGI Friday's, and I had a massive bowl of butter-laden angel hair pasta with garlic shrimp). And then one day he asked me if I'd like to go to an Easter cantata.

I don't remember if it was over the phone or in person, but I had never heard of a cantata. It sounded like *piñata*, so maybe I thought there were games like that involved. I don't remember asking what it was or if he explained that it was something like a musical. I think it was Good Friday. But I had no plans and no real reason to say no. I guess I figured, hey, why not?

# THE REVELATION

IT DIDN'T LOOK like a church. Pastor Phil had called it an *Easter* cantata, and so I guess I expected stained-glass windows, long straight rows of wooden pews, and a massive cloth-draped altar. This looked more like a junior high with a large open room that seated maybe three hundred, the two of us somewhere close to the back-center section of seats, at the end of one row. It was all so ordinary, neither fancy nor tacky, no one really dressed up or dressed down, a casual but not too casual atmosphere. You felt welcome and comfortable, but it didn't feel like church as I had always known it.

It was the same old story I knew pretty well, though never so up close and personal. The same familiar characters and setting fleshed out into vivid facial features, conversations, head coverings and flowing robes, shields and spears and shepherd's staffs. The culture clash of Jew and Roman, men and women, poor and rich, slave and free—moral and immoral, powerless and powerful. It all absorbed you, led you right along with all the rabble hanging on the every word the peaceful Rabbi spoke, his parables so plain but full of truth and mystery. His tenderness, compassion, sympathy toward the down and out. And yet not all were so enthralled by him. How could they be, whose power-hungry, money-loving motives he exposed? How plain it was to see that hating him would never satisfy their ends. Hate by itself wouldn't make him go away. And so of course the lovely songs and solos soon enough gave way to darker, more discordant ones. A tall dark shadow shaped like a cross appeared against one empty wall, and underneath it, on his knees, the staunch centurion, who'd watched and even taken part in the mockery, arrest, and beatings, sang. No sooner had the Rabbi breathed his last than this bold soldier gasped: "Truly this man was the Son of God."

And truly it was entertaining for an hour or so. A pleasant evening out. Until those final moments, when time stood absolutely still and Jesus Christ of history became as real to me as I or anyone in the room. More than just a name I'd memorized some things about. An actual human being of flesh and blood, who, as the Scriptures say, lived down here once upon a time, who really ate and drank and laughed and cried and let himself be crucified. But more than that, another deep conviction couldn't be denied, that I was part of why he came from heaven to earth to die. Something I'd known, but never known like that. In part because I couldn't run and hide in all the usual ways, nor strangely did I even want to try. Like hordes of locusts blackening the sky, a steady swarm of all the things I'd said and done throughout the years engulfed my mind. To which I was surprised that in my own defense I had nothing to say. Just tears of shame and hope of what seemed just as clear a conviction as the first: that my debt had long before I'd ever known or cared been paid, and if I would I could be reconciled.

And how refreshing that it didn't matter that I hadn't crossed and dotted all my T's and I's. There was no *But you need to do this first*. And in that light it felt as natural as breathing just to bow your head and close your eyes. Confession never flowed so freely. Guilt never felt so stripped of all its pride. I knew not what to say but just surrendered there my soul and will and mind. Somehow I muttered something like: "I've lived for myself long enough. I don't care what it means—from here on out I want to follow You." And in that moment all my hopelessness and fear about the future fled—and in their stead a deep and all-consuming peace remained.

# BORN AGAIN

IT HAPPENS IN a moment and thereafter you're never the same. Maybe the same could be said of other experiences, but this one is in a league of its own. After all, it's the eternal Spirit of the Living God you receive, the infinite within the finite. Although it doesn't make you God—just one with Him somehow, and yet distinct. It's a mystery, but it doesn't hurt to talk about. Jesus said you must be, if you would enter his Kingdom. He said the wind blows where it wishes, and you hear the sound of it, but you don't know where it comes from or where it's going—so it is with everyone who is born of the Spirit. It only happens once, and it might be dramatic or very ordinary, though in every case it is extraordinary, and lasting peace and joy are instant byproducts. Not something you effect at your own discretion, any more than you can control the wind, though to some degree you participate. You say, "Yes." It's impossible to say what each one feels, but I feel sure that each experience is unique, inasmuch as is each individual. It matters not if you are white or red or black or young or old or rich or poor or sharp or dull; a rule-keeper or breaker of them all. Everyone is equally unqualified and undeserving, not to mention unprepared. There you are going about whatever it is you are doing, and suddenly you see what you didn't before. Your eyes are opened and Jesus Christ becomes much more to you than just a name. And forever thereafter you're never the same.

# EPILOGUE

Being baptized, 2003

Pastor Phil and I, 2015

# THE CHANGE

THE FIRST REALLY telling, tangible thing was the peace. Not just a momentary peace as I prayed that evening, but the kind that sticks with you—*closer than a brother*, as the song says. What the Bible calls *the peace that surpasses all understanding*. I left that auditorium a different person, circumcised in heart. And I sometimes wonder if I was the only one who left there so changed. Suddenly it was okay to be in the wheelchair. It was okay even to look into the future a ways. Everything was okay after that.

The Bible says it best: death to life, darkness to light, blindness to sight.

Another thing too clear to miss was the inner war with the former status quo. It was surprising, actually, to find right off the bat that most of the music and movies I had so loved really grieved the new Life within me. Whether it was the vulgarity or overall tone or something I couldn't quite put my finger on, the Life within recoiled, and the peace. And it came down to a simple choice: either part with the thing or part with the peace. The longer I neglected it, the hotter the convictions burned. So week by week and one by one, I started first by taking down the empty liquor bottles we had been collecting like trophies, which lined the tops of the kitchen cabinets. And along these lines no rock was left unturned. Some things were gone within a week, while others took months or even years. But right away I knew that I was done with chew and booze and pot for good. And I've never looked back.

Not that the Christian life is mainly a matter of *Thou shall not*. Far from it, despite how many live that way. It is certainly a life of surrender, and there are guiding principles and warnings given by both the Spirit and the Book to point out wrong directions from the right. But it's not about depriving yourself, for whatever reason, least of which to try to prove your worth or earn your way. That kind of hopeless slavery may be called religious or spiritual, but it's not Christian. It isn't that *everything* from the "old life" is bad, necessarily, in itself. It's just that with some things it takes some time to notice how they make you think and feel and act, to see if they are hindrances or contradictions of the Life and Book. I'd had my fill of all the same old song and dance that only leaves you empty in the end. I'd squandered too much time the way it was. So if it grieved the Life within, it had to go.

That's the amazing thing to me about those few short months before I moved. Though it never crossed my mind, it was concrete proof that God exists (not that I needed further proof). I'd only just begun to read the Book, so I had no clue what it said about how to live. The Spirit within alone was guiding me. My new friend Phil encouraged me to start to read a chapter a day, beginning with the gospel of Luke. I remember starting in Genesis back in seventh or eighth grade, and maybe making it to chapter three. But that's as much as I'd ever read, except for the verses we'd memorized in confirmation class, the bulk of which were long forgotten. So for a week or two Phil stopped by, and we'd read together and discuss and pray. And after that I was pretty much on my own.

So many take for granted that they've always had the Life of God within. They were born with it, they think, or got it shortly after birth through some religious ritual. Or they presume beliefs are handed down from parents like an heirloom, and it's conferred upon a person automatically. Not that some don't come to know God at an early age or less dramatically. Not everyone has such a radical turnaround. Our stories are as varied as the constellations, clouds, or flowers. But to take it for granted just because seems hardly wise in any case.

As with the injury, I've lived both sides. Whose woods these are I thought I knew—and then I found out differently. I'd rather people didn't have to make the same mistakes I did before discovering what they don't now see. But what can you do? Sometimes it takes a tragedy to wake us from the slumber that we're in.

# THREE PERSONS, ONE ME

ONCE UPON A time I was normal. I lived a normal life. It was all I knew. Taking for granted that one perspective. There's the genetic side, beyond our choice entirely. The where and when and to whom we are born. The choices we make and the choices others make that impinge on us. All our highlights and lowlights. They're all part of the puzzle of the equation of who we are.

It's funny how there have been three of us now living in this body. That's how I tend to think of it, anyway, though there are different ways of drawing the lines. Three very different versions of myself, so far. The me apart from Christ and wheelchair; the me in wheelchair, apart from Christ; the me in Christ, and Christ in me, in wheelchair. Each time a radical reformation and reconstitution of who I was and am. Each time I chose and didn't choose who I'd become. Three different personalities. Three totally different lives. Two cataclysmic changes in three years. One me.

Outside a miracle, I'll never know how life past nineteen feels in an able-bodied frame. I'll never think or feel from that perspective. I'll never become that version of myself. Nor will I ever know, had the injury happened earlier or later than it did, or not at all, how strangely different hindsight might appear. How strangely different everything might be.

# PLAYING GOD

PEOPLE ASK IF I miss being able to do the things I used to, or what I miss most. Usually I say basketball and driving, for starters. I still dream of basketball and sometimes try to imagine what it might feel like to dribble or shoot three-pointers or drive the lane again after so long. It's amazing, really, what an impression even the simplest things can make on you. The feel of grass or sand or even mud between your toes. Being able to reach and scratch most every itch. Holding the door for ladies or for those who need a hand. Blending in most everywhere you go. The steady rhythm of a casual stride, snapping your fingers as you go. Collapsing into bed and getting right back up again. Running errands, doing dishes, sweeping floors, raking leaves, mowing lawn, shoveling snow. Working up a good sweat. Sign me up. I'll be your hunky-dory lackey for the day. No charge.

But I don't miss it all the way I used to. Back when remembering hurt so much. It's nice to enjoy the memories for what they're worth and not want anything more than them. Not everyone is so fortunate. Most people are shocked when I say I wouldn't go back and change things if I could. If we lived in a world where wishes came true, and it were possible with a single stroke of willpower to turn back the clock and change the way a certain something happened (what an uncertain and terrifying world that would be!). If you had asked me twenty years ago, I would have answered differently. But I've lived enough now that I can say I'm thankful that I've had to walk a road less traveled by. You learn things that you couldn't learn otherwise.

What if, after horsing around with my buddy that morning, I had gotten up as usual and continued at my job? There is the temptation to add: *and then gone to college and got a degree and found a wife*, and on and on. What then? As much as I might have wanted any one of those, in that particular context, to be givens, they never were. Not even for a second. And who's to say that path would've held more promise than the one that I've been on? If right this minute my body started working the way it did before, I might do a hundred things I can't do now. I might jog to the Y and shoot some hoops, in fact, or hop in the van and take a drive. And like it or not, whatever choice I make affects a million other things in ways that I could never guess, for better or worse. Moment by moment, our lives are balanced on this razor's edge—contingency upon contingency. And who are we to say that things would be put right if only this or that had happened differently?

# SPARED

THOUGH IT'S POINTLESS and irrelevant, I like to think that I've been spared from circumstances worse than these. That if the injury hadn't happened exactly as it did, and when—and ditto with how and when I was drawn to Christ—I might have done things which I might have never thought that I could ever, or would ever, do. A string of huge mistakes with consequences larger still. Which would have affected others, too, of course, and set in motion chain reactions that I couldn't undo. A lot of anger, bitterness, embarrassment, and shame might have been caused. It's purely speculation. There's only One who truly knows for sure, though even in eternity perhaps He'll never make it known.

# SHARING THE STORY

WHEN I ENTER the room, I sit silently off to the side of the students, watching them mill around and chat and fiddle with their papers and books. Several of them glance at me and we exchange smiles. Young ladies mainly, a lot of single mothers, for the most part under thirty though a few over forty. Every now and then a renegade male or two among them. They are Certified Nursing Assistants in training, a class offered through the local Adult Education office.

My friend, their teacher, has asked me to come and share "my story" again. I get an e-mail from her every six months or so and always say yes. After making a couple preliminary announcements, she introduces me and explains how we met—my first job out of college—teaching rudimentary English to non-native English speakers as part of a grant through that same Adult Education office. And then she turns me loose, and I have as long as I want to tell them whatever I feel like, which is always more or less the same. I can even mention Jesus if there is an opportunity. It's a learning moment for them. A chance to hear the personal side of healthcare, straight from the horse's mouth.

So I usually start right back at the ball fields that rainy morning way back when. Then lead them one experience at a time through the six months at Sioux Valley, seven months at my parents', nine months at Courage, fifteen-odd months in New Brighton, and then on to Marshall. I'm not shy about sharing humiliating experiences or demonstrating my lack of strength and dexterity. I talk about ventilators and enemas and blood clots and pressure sores and catheter bags and blitzkriegs. I want to help them help others in my shoes, and so I don't hold back. I tell them not to be afraid to ask me anything at all. Without fail, someone always asks about "the friend you were wrestling with"—*how is he doing, and are you still friends? Did you ever struggle with depression or accepting the injury? Are you married? Do you live alone?* We conclude whenever they stop asking, and all told it usually takes anywhere from half an hour to forty-five minutes. Then Vickie thanks me and I make my way for the door, but not before a good many of them smile and clap and say the same.

I'm always surprised by people's reactions. To me it's just my ho-hum life and history, which I share very matter-of-factly. Yet for years now, in a variety of settings, large or small, it hasn't escaped my notice that people often come away impacted. Sometimes you see tears stream down their faces. Expressions and shoulders go suddenly limp. Even in the grocery store or at work or church as you go about your everyday activities, people are curious how you wound up in such a condition, especially when you're under forty. The fact that you so freely smile and laugh also throws them for a loop. And whether trembling or fearless, they ask. A child of even four or five will blamelessly look you in the eye and say, "Why don't your legs work?" or "Why are your hands like that?" And you, usually caught off guard, learning as you go, try your best to explain to them the nuts and bolts of your life. And in a funny way sometimes you feel a bit like the mother bird chewing up worms into portions suitable for the little ones. Even the older ones can hardly believe that something so unexpected and life-changing could happen to someone—anyone—in a split second. As my roommate at Courage used to say, "A disability is a heartbeat away."

Probably the most shocking thing is hearing someone occasionally say, "You're such an inspiration," or "Have you ever thought of writing a book?" It happened just the other night, at an annual community event, where I saw a friend from college that I hadn't seen in years. We were just sitting down to eat, and I was nonchalantly fumbling with the Velcro splint I wear that holds my fork, and he said to me, "Ted, you're an inspiration to me." Just like that, the first thing out of his mouth. Apparently that's all it takes to be inspiring! And what are you supposed to say to that? It blindsides you and leaves you mumbling something half-incoherent.

*A book?* you think to yourself. *Isn't that going a little too far?* But after hearing it enough times you start to wonder. On the other hand, the skeptic within tends to prune with its reasonable objections any latent optimism: *What's so special about* your *life?* And so you're not quite sure where that leaves you. In my case it left me asking the Lord for His thoughts on the matter.

Sometime after that, my friend Joy from Ivory Coast asked if I'd be willing to correspond by phone with a friend of hers in order to give her practice speaking English. I agreed, and a couple years down the road, during one of our conversations, this newfound friend very matter-of-factly and out of the blue happened to say, "Do you know that you will write a book?" Not "Have you ever thought about it?" but "You will." This from someone I'd never met, whose English at the time was in its infancy. But the certainty in her tone never wavered, which reminded me that the friend who initially connected us had mentioned that prophecy happened to be one of her Christian giftings. So she would hear none of my unremitting doubts and protests, maintaining that she was as convinced of it as she was of her own name. But that didn't help me. I had no clue what to write about, and therefore little motivation. Writing a book would be a lot of work. It would also mean putting a lot of ideas out into the public square, where you influence everyone who comes into contact with them, for better or worse. So I felt I needed my own assurance that it was truly God's will for me. So I continued waiting and praying.

A few years later, tired of waiting and praying and limping back and forth between two opinions, I pleaded with the Lord for a long time one evening for a clear answer one way or the other. Before bed, I checked the mail and found a large manila envelope with a familiar return address: Valparaiso, Indiana. Suddenly I remembered a fairly recent e-mail from my Aunt Gloria, saying that she and my Uncle Bob had each written up their own brief testimony of what Christ had done in each of their lives in the midst of a decade of unexpected health problems, which they had presented at a retreat and then sent my way. A short, handwritten note was attached to this stapled packet of typewritten pages, the first line of which I could hardly believe: "Have you considered writing *your* story?"

# SOME MEMORIES

THIS AFTERNOON I'M sitting outside, and it's sixty-one degrees and sunny, the first week in March. People are out and about everywhere you look with a noticeable spring in their step. There's a young lady pushing a stroller; a pair of nurses from the nearby clinic with swinging arms and steps in tandem; rollerbladers, skateboarders, couples holding hands. The first thing on everyone's lips is recognition of the obvious, instant common ground.

I've found the spot on the south end of the building near the grill that is blocked off from the light breeze, though it still dances over my skin now and then, just enough to keep me cool. I'm wearing a long-sleeved layer of Under Armour ColdGear under a split-pea-soup–colored lambswool turtleneck, and it's just right. I spot one of my neighbors with MS—there are four now that Bev died—with one of her caregivers, who is piloting the joystick of her chair as they make their way down the block. Half an hour later they return and veer my way.

The caregiver is giggling at me, and I'm pretty sure I know why. It's a running joke with us, how it's finally nice enough for me to sit outside again, a sure sign that spring has arrived, like spotting your first robin. Somehow we get to how many layers I've got on—she's in a single T-shirt— and when with a smirk I say, "Just two," she tips her head back, rolls her eyes, and laughs her hearty laugh (I can always make her laugh). "That's down from the usual three or four," I tell her—always the Under Armour, often followed by a mock turtleneck and wool sweater. Depending on how cold and windy, the sweaters get multiplied, five layers total being the max; otherwise I need help getting my hat on and off. Usually I don't go without a coat when it's below zero, but after a couple months of having someone help me put on yet another layer over all the others—and a bulky one at that—I just grin and bear it. People ask why I don't move south. I don't think it's because I'd miss the changing seasons, though maybe I would. It's more my family and friends and church, and the fact that traveling isn't as easy as it used to be. I couldn't exchange them for warmer temps. I love it hot, but not that much. They are well worth a lifetime of brutal winters.

The briskness of the air out here brings back a sunny afternoon at Sioux Valley years ago, who knows what month, maybe September or October. It must've been about this cool and almost no breeze. One of the orderlies had rolled my bed out onto an open upstairs balcony. My only memory is lying there covered in blankets, the dry air and sunshine, barely warm, alive on my face. I hadn't been outside since that rainy morning back in June. Perhaps the sense of freshness I felt was like the difference you feel as you come out of the womb. It might have even brought back thoughts of days of getting out into the open air nearly every day, in the scalding heat or pouring rain or bitter cold. To miss a day of getting out in those days would have seemed like absolute torture. Yet so many days had passed in that ICU without my notice, except when from time to time I glanced out the window at the dismal rain drops streaming down against a background of dark clouds. I'd never been so cooped up in all my life. But that brief dose of fresh air and sunshine out on that balcony breathed some much-needed life into me, I think.

Which brings to mind another afternoon in the fresh air and sunshine, this time at Courage Center, when I first discovered one of the hallmarks of the quadriplegic. It might've been in the eighties or nineties, I don't quite remember. And humid, very probably August. It was always funny how many quads would be out there huddled together like turtles. I might've been out in it two or three hours, and when I came in lightheaded and nauseous, I wondered what was up. All I remember drinking in those days, besides a little milk at meals and an occasional pop, were the four-ounce juice cups with tinfoil tops, maybe three or four a day. When eventually the nausea got worse and a minor migraine took hold, someone mentioned something about overheating—didn't I know what that was? *Like a car?* I knew less about cars than quadriplegia at that point, but I was still able to make the connection. Surely people had told me I needed to drink plenty of water and avoid too much sunshine, since most quads no longer sweat, unless something's wrong. But good luck trying to keep me out of the sun.

I've always loved the sunshine. Not just the brightness and beauty of a clear blue sky, but more than anything that unmistakable sensation on the skin. There's a picture of me in just a diaper with Uncle Bryce holding me by the hands in shallow water at Roy Lake, big smiles on both our faces. So it probably started early. We almost always worked with our shirts off at the baseball fields, our dark hides glistening with tanning oil, and some afternoons the girls would drive by slowly and honk, and some of us would smile and pose and wave and flex.

Most cloudy days I struggle for the motivation to be productive. I often close the shades and turn on all the lights, two of which are high-wattage halogens. I don't remember being this way before the injury. Maybe it's that Seasonal Affective Disorder that people sometimes suggest when I'm moaning about the gloom, though I hate the idea that there's a diagnosis for everything these days.

Or maybe I've just developed a tolerance over the years, and my body craves it more than before. That wouldn't be so hard to believe. There's a community room I call the sunroom about fifteen feet from my apartment that's full of windows on three sides, and that gets me through the winters. I even get a slight tan, which surprises people. But from the time it hits sixty-plus (and low wind) I'm outside as much as possible, since summer slips away so quickly. No more taking off my shirt like the old days, though, to savor the feeling and hear people remind me how skinny I am.

I'm reading a book on memoir, and the creative sap is starting to flow. Something unusual is in process, though I'm not sure exactly what. Loose ends seem to be coming together, like a swirl of dried leaves stirred into a dust devil by just the right convergence of breezes. Just behind me, somewhere over my head, there's a subtle sound like tangled deer antlers, which I soon realize is the clanging together of bare tree branches, which reminds me that before long there will no longer be the clacking but more of a rustling. Then the image of rooftop sunshine at Sioux Valley returns, as well as that of the sultry afternoon at Courage.

I inhale deeply through my nose, stare off into the distant sky, and hold them all fast in my mind's eye, wondering what binds them all together. It seems to me they are themselves three leaves whose stems I hold between my forefinger and thumb. All roughly the same color and shape, all experiences of sunshine and fresh air—past and present fixed between my forefinger and thumb, the future pouring over me one thought upon the next, off and away into a vast reservoir somewhere behind me. But all this without the computer in front of me to get it down before it's gone. I could jot down a couple snippets of shorthand in my two-handed, half-legible scrawl, but that is painfully slow going and sometimes inhibits the flow, so I repeat the key ideas until I'm satisfied they're mine (which nine times out of ten fails, and you'd think I'd learn my lesson, but you know how that goes—so that by the time I get upstairs I can't be sure if there had been a sundog overhead; if so, it crowned a somewhat hazy sky of feathery clouds, with an unusually wide-brimmed halo).

Then, a little reluctant, I let them go, and as I do a poem comes in their place. A triolet. Iambic tetrameter. Phil Dacey's class. Fifteen years ago already.

> *Some memories are meant to fade,*
> *As leaves lose color and detach.*
> *One season finds us ill, dismayed;*
> *Some memories are meant to. Fade,*
> *The cruelest word, fierce as a blade—*
> *Sometimes a gouge, sometimes a scratch.*
> *Some memories are meant to fade,*
> *As leaves lose color and detach.*

# LOSING IT

A STRANGE THING crossed my mind one day. I might've been thirteen or fourteen at the time. I came across a business card from Mom's flower shop and tucked it into one of the chambers of my wallet, thinking that if someday I ever lost my mind and wandered away somewhere, I'd have it there to help me get back home. I always laugh when I think of it, in particular because I was so serious about it. Somehow I was under the impression that you could be going about your business one day as usual and suddenly, inexplicably, lose your mind, if that's how it works. I don't suppose I thought it through too thoroughly, but of course anything could happen, and in that case I wanted to be prepared.

Then one day I lost it. Not my mind—hallelujah!—but all I'd lived for. Gone forever in a moment. And for a long time there was no card or anything else to help me find my way back home.

It's interesting to think that we're always losing some of who we are, however slight or insignificant. Certain parts have to slip away to make room for the change in us, for better or worse. Maybe it's something like the rings of a tree, the new copied right over the old, and some of the way we once were is still hidden among a volume of such layers. It's amazing how we hold together, the same old us that stays the same in ways while changing constantly, sometimes drastically, by choice and not by choice.

Likewise, it doesn't seem like we have a choice of what we can or can't remember—in ways, yes, but absolutely, no. The fabric that connects us to our memories is so delicate, dependent on more than we know, much more than simply our power of recall. There are things we'd love to recall that we can't, and others we'd love to forget but we can't. And many probably, too, that we don't even know that we'd love to recall or love to forget. It makes me wonder what fills the void forgotten memories leave. On the other hand, there's a system working in there somehow, exquisite and far from random but not completely at our beck and call either. There is some good and bad in what we lose, and likewise also in what we retain.

# HOLDING SOMETHING
# I DON'T

IN *THINKING ABOUT Memoir*, Abigail Thomas shares a brief anecdote of her third hound, Carolina, proudly prancing around the yard for two days with a dead squirrel in her mouth. She absolutely wouldn't part with the thing. Until, eventually, she had to come into the house for supper, when the hand that holds the door took that opportunity to slip out and toss it into the bushes, out of reach. It's just one example of the gift she has for locating in everyday circumstances sometimes elusive realities. In this case, "someone you love holding something you don't."

I have a friend who is dying of drink. We barely knew one another growing up but got unexpectedly reacquainted recently through Facebook (imagine that). He's compelled, stalked by ghosts of the past—regret and guilt, irretrievable loss—which drink does drown, for the moment. It surprised me that someone would cling to what hurts; would even refuse to consider a cure. It took a while to read between the lines. Always the same sob stories, same litany of reasons, savoring something to lament. The love of pain for the love of drink. That was the revelation, though it's nothing new. Simply the means to the end.

I am one of the reasons—the fact that I wound up like this. He can't understand and won't let go. So he curses the fact nearly every time we talk, even blaming himself, he who had absolutely nothing whatsoever to do with it—in prison when it happened, I think he told me—rehashing the same script over and over, that I was a "good guy" and didn't deserve it, that I could've been happy and met someone and had a family and all the rest of it—that he would take my place, if only he could. He has no barometer for how it all might affect someone in my shoes, though I try in vain to reassure him that I *am* happy and satisfied with my life, that marriage and family, while still possibilities, would not be the center of my joy anyhow. Years ago I might have agreed with him and can imagine the weight of it all bearing down on me once the lights went out. But I'm not going back there for anything. I haven't arrived yet, but I've moved forward, and though there is sadness in the realization that he may not, at least now I know why. Though often sincere and well-intentioned in his sympathy, he's in love with the dead squirrel in his mouth.

I'm sometimes surprised that the aftershocks of the injury are still being felt—and often so keenly—twenty

years later. I'm surprised some still think of me as a victim.
Maybe it's naive to think it should be otherwise. My sister
tells me there were days when Mom would now and then
pull out the pictures of my shriveled frame in the halo vest
and weep her eyes out. We couldn't understand why she'd
put herself through that, but then neither of us is a mother or
a parent. My old friend Tom says there's not a day that goes
by that he doesn't think about me and what happened. He
watches his boys being boys and can't imagine "What if?"
I sometimes think he got the worse end of the deal. I take
mostly for granted that the injury doesn't hold me captive
anymore. I've all but forgotten how it feels to lie awake at
night and wonder hopelessly what the future holds. In some
ways I've lost touch with how hard letting go can be. But
still, I understand. Unique as we all are, we grieve and sort
through things so differently, and on different timetables.

For some the pain got buried years ago and sometimes
turns up uninvited when they least expect. And they have
their ways of keeping it in check. But it can only be put off
so long. And some, for whatever reasons, still hang on. It
makes no sense to cling to pain, but we're not such simple
creatures, either. There's a law at work in all of us that
always wants its way. A subtle law that isn't always rational,
that we serve more often than we like to admit. Maybe
some are just unsure what letting go might mean. Maybe
they're afraid there won't be anything or anyone to which
or to whom to cling.

# LUCKY LOCKEY
# AND AIR JORDAN

I<small>F YOU SAT</small> down with my sister and me and asked us to give you a ten-minute summary of some of our most interesting adventures over the past ten years, I'm afraid you'd find hers a lot more numerous and compelling than mine. She's got a lifetime of stories to draw from even just from her travels, while I have followed in my Dad's footsteps of being a notoriously humdrum homebody. And yet several years ago it so happened that I got the opportunity—if you can call it that—for an adventure that is hard to top and with which I'm sure I'll be amazing and horrifying people for years to come.

Lockey's legally blind and lives on the first floor. Many people mistakenly call him Lucky the same way they call me Todd or Tom or Tim. He used to stay in one of the corner apartments on the south side of second-floor, but after what happened the powers that be arranged for him to be moved down to first, lest history repeat itself. Every now and then he walks with his long white cane, but most of the time he motors around in his scooter, from one end of town to the other at all hours of the day, usually with his dog alongside him on a leash. Sometimes you even see him venturing out in subzero temps with a good amount of snow on the ground. In the fifteen-plus years I've known him, he's been hit by a car at least twice. He has to hold paper right up to his face to see it, even with the print enlarged, and yet sometimes he recognizes me from twenty feet away, which always confounds me.

So, it was a sunny summer afternoon, and I was just pulling into the lobby on my way upstairs for a routine refill on water. I passed Lockey by the mailboxes on my right and continued into the elevator, pressing the button for third floor, when he called out for me to hold it for him. I quickly backed my chair up to block the door from closing, and a few seconds later he pulled up behind me. There wouldn't have been room for both of us if I had pulled in parallel to the button panel, as usual, so I veered slightly left and straight ahead into the corner, parked diagonally, and he drove straight in behind me until he bumped into the wall, with maybe an inch between the back of my chair and his, and likewise between the backrest of his chair and the elevator door. My compromised position only allowed me an over-the-shoulder backwards glance out the corner of my left eye, but he appeared to fit. Then I noticed Jordan, his black Lab-Dalmatian mix, which I'm not sure I saw with him on my way in. He was trying to poke his head in behind Lockey, just to the left of his chair, between us, but there wasn't room. So he retracted his paw and tried the right side, with the same result, and stepped back again. And no sooner did his long snout cross the threshold than the shiny silver door slid slowly and smoothly past him, pinning his leash to the wall.

*No, that didn't just happen,* I thought to myself.

But it did. The door was shut and the button was lit, and Jordan was outside and we were inside, and even if I could have reached it, which I couldn't, it was too late. The leash was tied to Lockey's chair, and the elevator was starting to move. Worst of all, I heard a whimper, and the sound of Jordan's sixty-plus-pound frame slamming up against the door and starting to slide—up, of all things, quickly up the wall.

Be thankful you can't hear the sounds which ought not to be heard—which never were before, perhaps, nor ever will be again, let's hope—the untamed thrashing, gasping, whining, gagging, banging back and forth against the door. Directly followed by the subtle chime for second floor, when Lockey's chair shot just as suddenly back into the door, so hard it tipped the front end in the air, jerking us to a standstill with a hollow-booming roar.

"Jordan?" Lockey pleaded softly. "Jordan? Jordan?"

Again, my stomach sank. I, the button-pressing fool. How guilty, I can't say. A fleeting spark of hindsight said I should have waited 'til I knew for sure. But there was no time for that. No wishing it away or going back. I pressed the button I could reach, the only one that could do us any good. Five or six or seven times, maybe more, I pressed it, an ear-splitting school-bell racket that always makes me jump. When after a minute no one came, I kept on pressing it. And then, below it, I spotted the thin steel door that hides the phone, and with one knuckle nudged it open.

"You'll have to grab it," I told Lockey. "Just dial 911!"— which by some miracle he did.

How long did we sit there listening and waiting— listening and waiting, listening and waiting? It must've been a few minutes at least just for the struggle, then maybe another five or more in silence once the restless legs gave out (ever so reluctantly, I assure you). That might've been the worst part—toenails scraping steel so fervently you thought they might slice through. I kept wondering what the door must look like out there, its lavender paint all ripped to shreds. I thought they might even need an entirely new one. I never did like the lavender anyway.

Though I'm not usually so inclined, I couldn't resist praying for poor Jordan. I remember praying for our first cat, Morris, as a kid when now and then he got himself lost for a week or more. That qualified as a bona fide crisis. And I prayed for my cat Chuck after I gave him away so long ago for the sake of a girl I nearly married (I felt so guilty I even wrote a poem in his memory). Whether it was during or after the struggle, I don't know. I only know I bowed my head and closed my eyes and silently begged the God of mercy on behalf of His poor creature—Lockey, in particular.

Meanwhile, our building caretaker passed by the elevator on his way through the lobby and did a double take at the long limp spectacle hanging in plain sight. He'd been painting an empty room on second floor and heard the furious alarm bell. Quickly he pulled out his pocket razor and cut the leash, and Jordan hit the floor with a solid thump. Then, inexplicably, this heavy lump of dog did something else. He bounced right back up on his feet, shook his head back and forth a few times, sneezed, pooped a single turd, and took off running.

It might have been that Lockey was confusing someone on the other end of the line with a shaky mouthful of strange and scattered details when the number of voices below us seemed to increase, the elevator chimed again, and we began to descend. The door opened to a swollen semicircle of curious faces, including a couple of emergency responders, who never look surprised. I can't imagine having come out of there to poor Jordan lying in a silent heap—and worse, Lockey's reaction. I'm not sure what that might have done to me.

To this day it remains my most traumatic life experience. I don't have flashbacks or anything like that, though, inside or outside elevators, nor even a fear of elevators. On the other hand, it contained a miracle. Two, in fact. The elevator door somehow escaped without even the faintest trace of a scratch. Three or four excruciating minutes of bone-chilling scratching, and nothing. I was astounded.

I have a friend who laughs his head off every time the story comes up. I tell him if he had been in there with us he wouldn't have been laughing. Even Lockey laughs about it now, though, so if he can, I guess anyone can.

# NASOGASTRIC INTUBATION

THEY CALL IT an NG tube. Hospitals are full of such abbreviations. "We need to put in an NG tube," they say. And that doesn't sound so bad.

I don't remember the first time. Once is enough for a lifetime. The records say it was about a week after the injury, when I was under heavy anesthetic. They were having trouble keeping my lungs clear and, because of suspicions of pneumonia, were doing regular suctioning. A month or more later, there were at least one or two other times, as feeding tubes. And though by then the anesthesia had been greatly reduced, none of these conjures up any memories.

The last time, not so many years ago, my intestines were exceedingly swollen (they called it *megacolon*) and the tube was put in to suck out the excess gas. The second I saw it in the nurse's hands and remembered where it was going, I kept telling myself I'd rather die than go through it again. I may have even told her so. But she just stood there looking at me indifferently and probably said something to reassure me ("Come on, you little pansy, make up your mind," is what she looked like she was thinking). At which I imagine I sighed and gave her the okay. And before I could change my mind, she dipped the flimsy thing in clear jelly and stepped toward me.

By her every subtle movement you could tell she'd done this countless times and could probably do it blindfolded, which was both reassuring and unsettling. With one hand palming my forehead, she tilted my head back and I felt the cool and slimy tube—not quite thick as a pencil— slide quickly into one nostril and begin to penetrate the tiny opening in the back, which made me brace myself with wider eyes. She probably said "Relax," but my mind and body couldn't agree, thinking of the grossness of the jelly in there as it started to ooze down my throat, and the steady pain of the tube being forced through, which made me start to gag, like one prolonged dry-heave as she kept repeating, "Just keep swallowing." So against my will I obeyed, thinking, *Just get it over with*, as the thing snaked toward my gut.

"You can relax now," I'm sure she finally said. I felt utterly defeated, the long thing hanging from my nose like an enemy's flag.

Then, for the next week, there was the joy of interacting with everyone with this awkward monstrosity front and center, with a nice fat chunk of white tape to boot. I could only hope for no visitors, though alas there were a few. Even when the good news eventually arrived that the thing could come out, my enthusiasm was minimized by the sudden way the doctor slid it up and out, gagging me ever so slightly and leaving a slimy trail of bile in my nose and throat. At that point, reminding myself that I did the right thing and that it was for my own good didn't help much. Until I stopped pouting and reminded myself that things could be a lot worse.

# A LITTLE PERSPECTIVE

SOMETIMES I WAKE in the middle of the night, burning up. I sleep with an ultra-soft fleece blanket pulled up over my head, which makes for a cozy little cocoon most of the year. Everyone thinks I'm crazy, but this is how I'm most comfortable. I like it warm, and most nights I sleep straight through without waking at all, but now and again I need to escape.

I lie in the same position all night long. Most often on my right side with both knees bent up toward me, a pillow between them and my ankles. When the sore on my backside is healed—the same spot I've been dealing with for years now—I get the privilege of lying on my back now and then. It's right under the left hipbone, where all my weight is centered when I'm in my chair. Twice during the day I also lie down like this for an hour at a time, which has become more mandatory than ever in the last decade. It cuts into my work schedule and social life. The shallowest abrasion often takes months to heal, even when I'm eating right and lying down as often as I should. If the bandage I wear over the spot even when it's healed somehow gets folded over, or there happens to be a sizable wrinkle in my boxers or pants, and I sit on either of these for even just an hour or two, the wound can open up again. Most of the time I don't even realize it's happening, except sometimes part of my forehead suddenly starts to sweat, and I wonder what's going on, since that almost never happens. And then at the end of the day when my clothes come off we find out. The last one was the size of an eraser head, less shallow than a dime, and it took three years to mend, until we finally got my wheelchair cushion figured out (overinflating it is bad, it turns out, though so also is underinflating it). For a while it stays healed, and then before too long it opens again.

At any rate, with a couple nods of the head I nudge the fleece off my face enough to get a few breaths of fresh air, which is still stifling. With my left wrist, which is the stronger, I manage to wiggle under a fold of the blanket and toss it back a few more inches, which exposes my chest and brings a little more relief. It's a little darker than twilight, and there's no telling what time it is (the clock had to go years ago, as I tired of being reminded, at times like these, of how much sleep time I have left). My lips and mouth are parched, so I swish a little spit around to moisten them. I'm groggy enough that I actually think about getting up and opening a window, the wonder of a cool breeze pouring over my bare belly and thighs. Now and then I'll even find myself calling out, "Could you open a window?" only to realize a moment later that I'm alone. "Why didn't I have him open a window, or leave the fan on?" I scold myself. But the night I do that I wake up in a shiver, clinging to my precious blanket and pillow, murmuring, "Why didn't I have him shut that stupid window (or turn off that stupid fan)?"

The pillow, a folded up plush blanket that lies to the right of my face, is the problem. It's like having a warm, fat cat snuggled up beside you, which is nice most winter nights. So with my lips I nip at it lightly to get a grip, then with my teeth slide it right up next to my face, which brings to mind the image of multitudes of microscopic mites crawling all over my mouth, as with a sudden swing of my left arm I launch it up toward the pillow. Again, I wiggle my wrist under just enough of it to flip it back toward my legs, though sometimes it lands on my face or unfolds in the process, which is even hotter if it winds up getting stuck there. But usually it's still possible to flip it back again, over my chest and off the bed. And just like that it feels ten degrees cooler.

It feels even better to swing my left arm straight out and lay it beside me—at first. But quickly it feels warm again, and so I flip it onto my stomach, which is better, until it's not, and then it's back to my chest. For the next hour or more it keeps bouncing around this way every few minutes:

bed-belly-chest-bed-belly-chest-bed-belly-chest. When sleep won't take me back, there's nothing to do but try to let my mind and body rest, which actually takes a focused effort. In the center of the ceiling, the steady green light of the smoke detector flashes red every twenty-two seconds. In the other room, the computer is off, and for the time being the refrigerator, which means I can hear the clock out there ticking, as well as my breath. My mind flutters through a number of thoughts which repeat themselves over and over like the mantra of my restless hand, to the point that I have continually to tell myself to stop it and relax.

When it's dark and quiet and you're alone, you think differently than during the daytime. Things seem graver and less superficial. There's less distraction and more clarity. Things occur to you that don't during the day. I tend to make more resolutions at night, the day having passed and so many things left undone. At times the heat and darkness of a sleepless night make me think of hell—forever and ever, flames that never quench. Which makes the heat seem much more tolerable and sets me to praying for those I fear are on the fast track there.

Then there's the sound of scraping concrete in the parking lot next door—the snowplows, with their nearly constant *beep, beep, beep, beep, beep*. That makes it four or five a.m. Suddenly I think of the homeless huddled up out there—nowhere near, I'm sure, but somewhere. I thank God for the walls around me and the ceiling overhead.

Warm covers and a comfy mattress. The food on my table several times a day. At least one arm that works enough to allow me so much liberty in bed. The fact that I can breathe on my own without a machine and even live alone.

I'm telling you, there's nothing like a sleepless night to help put things in perspective.

# THAT SAYING

How DOES IT go? *Grow where you are planted?* Poking around online a minute, I find it, as well as its flipside: *You are not a tree. You don't need to grow where you are planted.*

There are two large plastic pots full of different kinds of flowers on either side of the brick pillars in front of the main entrance of my building. Just after summer started, an exceedingly windy storm cast many of them—mostly petunias—all over the pavement. They lay there for a while like corpses on a battlefield and no one seemed too eager to clean them up. But by the end of the week I noticed on different occasions three of them—one white, one purple, one pinkish—planted in the rock beds of two nearby trees. It had been in the eighties and nineties for several weeks, and yet they hung on there in apparently dry soil, at least on the surface. There was even one thriving in a sidewalk crack, which really floored me. You'd think someone planted them there just to get your attention, though their odd and random placements said otherwise. Who would plant a single flower in a sidewalk crack or bed of rocks?

They were blown there, or at least their seeds were, if one of the ladies who works in the building is right. There is hardly room for soil in a sidewalk crack, if you can even call it soil, which I imagine was in the same way as the seeds blown into it over time. Within a day or two, the purple one, which had more shade than the others, had become two purple ones, while the white ones were languishing, though I did my best to spit a few mouthfuls of water onto one of them. They're fierce little survivors, relatives of the tomato, I also found out. Here today and gone tomorrow. With and without help, they make the most of where they've been planted.

And I'd like to think that I do the same.

# ON BEING

PEOPLE TALK ABOUT their earliest memories: the smell of their favorite blanket or the color of carpet in their first house. I think mostly they are referring to images. Some say they were only two years old, or not even that, and they remember clearly. I wonder myself and close my eyes. The front window of my parents' living room appears, and outside the front yard filled with snow. Was this my earliest? If so, was I three or six? Or neither? After all, how many times have I seen snow through that window? A few images remain from preschool days, but they are fuzzy. Kindergarten is clearer, and the next few years slightly better, with the images, like snowflakes, piling up with each year. A handful of prodigies out there actually have photographic memories, and what a blessing and curse that must be. Even so, I'm a little skeptical of the certainty some claim along these lines. Some probably even claim to have memories from inside the womb. What seems remarkable to me about all this is not that it's possible many years later to recall our earliest memories—amazing as that is—but simply the rock-bottom fact of our self-consciousness or self-awareness. The miracle and majesty of being a living being.

To have come into being after not having been is an utterly mind-blowing thing, worthy of sincere reflection. It prompts the usual questions we all ask. We may wonder if it's even right to think in terms of *after* when we think of coming into being after never having been. (We came into being *after* we didn't exist?) We take so much for granted. Consider the simple fact of sperm and egg, and all the microscopic goings-on that happened to make up that much of who we are. That's one thing, and it's absolutely massive. But beyond the bare material there is soul and spirit, mind and will. However much we think we know as so-called modern men and women, these deepest things still keep us guessing.

Just think what a thing it is simply to be. Period. No one chooses to because no one can. Of this much we are sure. Yes, it seems obvious and nothing new. But how often do we ponder it as more than just a passing thought? The wonder of waking up conscious one day in the middle of somewhere for the first time—presumably looking up at someone sooner or later—the mind something of a blank slate, but not exactly blank, we seem to be learning. At that stage everything must seem like one big category, an indistinct potpourri of kaleidoscope impressions. Not that there isn't clarity soon enough. But right away how strange must be that ecstasy of sensory overload. Like sleeping, all is dark and warm and safe, until the monumental moment, slowly, we awake. And it's interesting—and not without significance, I'm sure—to note how sleep provides this way (in a sense) of being begotten afresh each day.

And more than this, it almost takes your breath away when now and then you realize your being. Or is it that you realize you're being? Beyond the fact that you're alive. You're looking in the mirror at your teeth or nose up close, going about your usual routines, and as you back away you stop, holding your pose, and linger long. There's suddenly someone staring back who wasn't there before—or so it seems—and you're gripped and feel the moment swell. It's being—a heightened sense of it—the gravity and eternity of who and what you are. In one sense it's a thing you have, but more. Not simply in the way of nouns, but more dynamically, in the way of verbs, a kind of "is-ness" or "ing-ness" that makes you smile and brings to mind a secret you forgot. And yet it isn't something that you do, but are, and you're happy you can't say exactly what it is or isn't. You only know you are and once were not, and it's clear you've only scratched the surface of some deeper truth. And the more you ponder it you're grieved at how so much is always going on around you, so many trifles clouding up the mind. No wonder the experience is rare. Which makes you wonder how your life might change if you were always so aware.

We should be thankful for the opportunity, though some might hesitate to call it that. Perhaps for them the womb was not the sanctuary it ought to have been. It may have been their enemy in ways they had no power change, though to some degree that's true of all of us. To have made it out at all—healthy and whole, no less, whatever that means—should never be taken for granted. If you've watched a young child sleep, you know how precious that peace is, and thus how holy a place the womb. Whatever we bring with us out of there, the rest is up for grabs. From there no matter where we go we're shaped, for better or worse.

The ones to whom I owe my natural birth each have three siblings. Each is special and unique in his and her own way. But they are aunts and uncles to me, not as much my flesh and bone. To have been born to one of them would have meant for each of us a different life—or, in other words, different states of being. The reasons why things happened as they did are many, I imagine, more than any of us could guess. Instead, the two who call me son were somehow drawn together and besides me bore another one. There were almost three, but the first, a he, a year before me, was not to be. The two who were have grown, and for countless reasons big and small these two have not begotten yet their own. Maybe they will eventually, or won't—and if they do, or don't, they will be shaped one way or other, for reasons big and small, in ways unique beyond what we could guess.

The One to whom I owe my second birth—the supernatural one—Himself had no beginning, nor will have an end of being. In Him the power to be has always been. This is the necessary mystery. For anything to ever come to be, there must be One behind it all Who has this power—Who is this power—to be.

# HOW I'LL GO

I WONDER IF I'll see it coming, like a car swerving into my lane at the last minute, or in the midst of the final symptoms of a drawn-out bout with cancer. There's something to be said for being blindsided when you least expect it. At any rate, it's not something we like to think about much. We don't know one way or other, and a little or a lot of thinking about it won't bring us any closer to knowing. But that doesn't mean we shouldn't think about it now and then or wrestle with the questions it brings up. *What is it that I'm really living for? Are there things that need to change in how I live my life?* Et cetera.

My friend Joe and I were talking about it just the other night. I was mentioning how people in general—myself included—tend to take for granted that they'll slip away peacefully during the night, probably at a ripe old age. Then again, I'm sure there are plenty out there who habitually live in fear of it, one way or the other. I remember more than twenty years ago dreaming on a regular basis of either being shot or strangled or falling from some great height (which ended once Jesus came in). None of us likes to think we'll go that way. "Dyin' ain't easy, hey," my friend replied, "the body fights it."

This brought to mind the times I'm often overcome with dizziness during the week. Either I haven't been drinking enough water, or I'm in the process of eating or talking with someone, or all of the above, and suddenly I can hardly see six inches in front of me. My tongue, facial and neck muscles start to feel weary, which makes it hard to talk. It feels best just to sit still and stop talking and breathe easy, trying in vain to push one hand against my legs enough to induce a spasm. This makes them squeeze together briefly, which helps the blood flow up from below my knees and brings a little relief. When there's someone with me, I ask them to move my knees back and forth, over and over, which we call *charging the batteries*, and that helps, as does drinking a good deal more water. "Are you okay?" people naturally ask. "This is normal," I murmur.

On rare occasions it happens first thing in the morning, in the shower, but more severely, to the point that my limbs feel pins and needles everywhere and things go whiter yet, and I can hardly hold my head up, and a gradual, involuntary panic is aroused—*I can't see, I need to go, back to bed, I can't see, I need to go, now, bed, now, now, now.* Almost instinctively, I start breathing deeply in and out, trying to imagine my kitchen table and bookshelf and doorjambs and hoping my toes don't get banged into anything as my caregiver quickly pushes me from bathroom to bedroom. It makes me wonder if I could handle blindness along with everything else, and I think probably not. My ears ring and I hear the belt around my waist being undone and feel myself being lifted from the chair. The moment I hit the mattress, a tremendous guttural sigh slips out, which sounds worse than it feels, and a wave of relief rolls over me, my forehead suddenly starting to feel cool and clammy. I continue the deep and steady breathing, lifting my head for a couple seconds at a time as the blood rushes upward and my eyes feel the pressure behind them build. The miracle of sight returns in multicolored patchy streaks, and I feel like I could sleep the rest of the day. But fifteen minutes later I'm all dressed and in my chair and on my way to work as if it never happened.

Maybe that's the way I'll go. That doesn't seem like such a bad way.

It could have easily been my time fifteen years ago, when I was hospitalized for a few days to kick a wicked bout of bronchitis and pneumonia, which included some scary nights of being held over the bed as I hacked and heaved until the tears rolled. A few years after that I hadn't gone to the bathroom for seven days and my innards were so distended that I would dry heave every time I took a drink of water—which meant another ER visit followed by a four-day hospital stay. There are blood clots that run the length of both my legs, and pretty much constant bladder infections and occasional pressure sores. And on any given day it could be any of those things or something else entirely, logical or illogical, that ends up being the means to carry me Home.

These days I usually call Mom and Dad every week rather than every two or three. I don't take them for granted the way I used to now that they are both over seventy-five, and I over forty. The more I live, the more I'm convinced that every day is a gift we dare not take for granted, and yet I still do. I remember hearing from a doctor that first year after the injury that a person in my condition and of my particular makeup might only live to see thirty-five. For whatever reason, it didn't faze me then, but I remember one of my buddies who was with me quickly wiping away a sudden tear. I think I'd be happy if I made it to fifty, though that's not too far off, so maybe sixty. It's hard to believe I've been in the chair now longer than I was out of it. And by the grace of God I've survived so much thus far. It's a beautiful thing to have no fear of death anymore, but I suppose that's easier said when you're not staring it directly in the face. At any rate, that's part of the joy and privilege of investing your trust in Jesus Christ, who not only pardons sin and cleanses conscience but offers the free gift of eternal life with Him. Which brings to mind a line from a song I love: *No guilt in life, no fear in death, this is the power of Christ in me.*

At any rate, I sometimes wonder what effect it might have on us all if we could only see how much we're being saved from every hour of every day.

# THIS LITTLE LIGHT

THERE'S A JOY and peace and certainty in the Christian life that you just can't explain, try as you may. This lasting joy and peace doesn't mean you always feel like doing jumping jacks or brightly smiling at everyone you see. It doesn't mean you never have the kind of days where nothing seems to go your way. It doesn't even mean that you're immune to doubt or stress or worry or tears. Among other things, it means that on days when you are caught off guard by the jaded questions of skeptics, you have this feeling deep within that you'd love to make plain to them, but it's not so easy. Especially in the early years. In any case, you do your best and usually feel that you have fallen short. You only hope and pray that what they see and hear from you is not what turns them off. It's just that you have Good News to share, and like all good news, it's hard to keep it to yourself. Selfish as we all are, we love to share the things we most enjoy. The trouble in this case is that the good news is pointless without the bad news first. That's just the nature of this news. And no one likes bad news, especially when it's bad news for them, personally—even sometimes when it's followed by good news. Most would rather hear bad news from their doctor than listen to this news, or at least sometimes that's how it seems.

"That's good for *you*," they often say, "if you *need* that." And I do. I really, really do.

Then what to do with this little light of mine? Hide it under a bushel? No! I'm going to let it shine!

But when I say that I *need* this News, or this faith, what do I mean? The word *need* is synonymous with *required* or *indispensable* and may even imply urgency. By definition, *need* means something which one cannot do without. But in what sense is this *need* of mine something I can't do without? In other words, what is the nature of this need—beyond a need to know what is actually true?

*All* truth has implications for how we live. Is it really true, as the Bible claims, that a living, personal, supernatural Being with powers greater than we can imagine exists, who always has and always will, who made all things, to whom we are all ultimately accountable? If so, and if it's also true that this Being who gave me life is Truth and Purity itself—perfect goodness, wisdom, justice, patience, mercy, love, and more—and all I am before Him is defiled, guilty, full of greed and need, then I find myself a debtor who owes Him more than I could ever pay. That's part of the bad news no one wants to hear. It says there's something wrong with me that *needs* to be put right. It says I *need* to be reconciled to the One from whom I was born estranged. The world is full of longing for it, the tireless search to fill the heart with everything but Him. That's why the ones who prize this News take pains to make it known—because they've found that it's not only true, but that it has the power to transform lives.

The other sense in which I have this need relates to how I handle the hardest situations that I face. This is the sense that many mean when they laugh at the idea of *needing* God. It's the same old tired tale of faith being more or less a crutch for fragile minds, the so-called "opiate" that many need to cope. I can only answer for myself. I tried to make it on my own and found myself in a dry and weary land. So much in life depends on just how much we're up against. It's only when we're stuck in a pit and our own resources come up short that we start to look beyond ourselves for help. For me there came a breaking point—a moment of truth—and a breakthrough. But I didn't believe because it soothed my pain (though it certainly did), or even because it promised to. I believed because I couldn't do otherwise, or so it seemed. The Truth before me was far too plain and couldn't be denied. In that moment I could sooner have denied that I exist.

This second sense of need includes how all things work together for my good. It's what the Bible promises concerning everyone who holds the faith, that everything that happens in my life—and "everything" means *everything*—God somehow causes to work together for good, according to His purposes and plans. The promise doesn't say I'll see or understand how something's working for my good. I'm simply left with promises to trust, or not to trust. This promise, in particular, is made in light of greater ones, whose gravity provides the ground for such an audacious claim. It's a well-known promise that, through the eyes of faith, becomes a kind of lens through which the baffling things are seen to make more sense. Call it a means to cope, if you must, as long as you don't assume that it's the only or primary reason I believe. It's simply one of the perks of Christian faith.

Some days it's not so easy, though, to believe that God is working everything together for my good. Now and then the tube of the drainage bag I wear along my leg gets kinked or somehow disconnected, and I wind up soaking wet, no matter if I'm home or at the store. Or I'm out having lunch with family or friends and suddenly get so dizzy I can hardly talk or see or finish my meal. So what do I do—force a smile and pretend it's not frustration that I feel? Hardly. But on the whole I trust my Bible, which says that we walk by faith and not by sight. I've learned firsthand that faith untested is brittle, at best—and possibly, at worst, not even genuine faith at all. Unpleasant as these things can sometimes be, they do nothing to negate the truth of promises that I and many others hold so dear. Sometimes we only learn years later—or months or days or hours—how something we once considered "bad" turns out to have been a blessing in disguise. Some of the deepest, dearest lessons I've learned have been in the midst of the longest, darkest hours.

There's so much we don't know—can't know—about the present moment in which we live, not to mention those ahead of us (both here and in the endless Age to come). I may not know how some "bad" thing is working toward my ultimate good, either now or in eternity. But since when do I need to know the how and why of every circumstance? Every choice I make sets off a chain reaction that, so far as I can tell, goes on and on and on in ways I have no power to trace. I only need to recognize one thing and settle down: my finitude. So the Christian really has no valid ground to doubt that all the "bad" in his life is actually being worked together for his good. I rest in knowing I'm part of a plan much bigger than myself.

One morning last winter I woke to a bedroom full of daylight, which meant my morning help, who normally comes at six, didn't show. Among other things, that meant that I couldn't make it in to work. I grumbled, sighed, and asked the Lord every few minutes why these kinds of things always have to happen, usually beyond my control. I wondered what the reason could possibly be, maybe a lesson I was supposed to learn. But mostly it seemed pointless. A total waste of time. When eventually my help arrived and I got up, I called the office to let them know what happened, and what a nice little surprise I had when they told me the furnace was out and they were all freezing their tails off. And there I had been all warm and cozy under the covers all the while, utterly clueless.

Make no mistake, the Lord of heaven and earth does truly work in mysterious ways.

# WHAT I'D DO

IF ONE DAY, while eating or reading or working or praying, I felt my thighs and calves alive with a fire I haven't felt in years, and looking down I lifted up one foot and then the other, bracing myself with hands and fingers that likewise suddenly started to work—mouth open, spreading wide into a smile, quick fits and starts of laughter sneaking out—then slowly rising off my cushioned seat and noticing each inch of altitude, the sensitivity of every joint, stepping here and skipping there, spinning, leaping, flailing my arms about. In tears, I'm sure. Perplexed and careless, carefree, all at once.

I've thought it through so many times. Especially in the early years. Less and less as time goes by. There's no sadness in it anymore. So sometimes I imagine, just for fun, although I'm not decided what I'd do. I'm sure whatever I think today is not what I thought ten years ago, nor even last year. Who can say what they'd do in a moment like that?

Would I run to all my neighbors first and boast, "Look— proof that Jesus heals!"? Then jump in the van and tell my friends from house to house, as well as everyone at work? Maybe I'd hop a plane to Brisbane and give my sister and Pete a happy shock. Most often, though, I think of Mom and Dad. They'd probably be the first. I'd love to make it a surprise, but Dad is over eighty now, and Mom not far behind, and I can just envision a fainting spell or worse. Probably better to call first.

"Something amazing happened!" I might say. "I'll be there in two hours. Make sure you're sitting down when you hear me honk." There'd be the same old sometimes tedious stretch of highways, full or empty fields of beans or wheat or corn or cattle, barbed-wire fences, farmsteads filling my mind in new and unexpected ways. And soon enough I'd be there in the driveway, wondering which door to use—not just the same old one out back with the ramp as usual. The one in front with the concrete steps is the one I always picture first—one slow, methodic step at a time. Or maybe I'd leap up in two swift strides? Then grasp the knob and twist and push—how long it's been!—and there they are, each on a separate sofa, waiting, possibly. Or Mom in the kitchen and Dad just walking toward me from his room. No matter where, they sit or stand there staring, like they have no clue who I might be—full height, a familiar face in baggy clothes. Would I try to speak and, failing, collapse and weep? Or stride or stagger toward them, or they toward me—our faces pressed together, arms entangled, groaning long and loud?

No matter how I picture it, it's always beautiful. It makes me smile and sometimes tears well up. It's possible. It's hope. And the best part is that if it never happens, it's okay.

Mom, Dad and I at Sarah and Pete's wedding reception, 2015

# listen|imagine|view|experience

## AUDIO BOOK DOWNLOAD INCLUDED WITH THIS BOOK!

In your hands you hold a complete digital entertainment package. In addition to the paper version, you receive a free download of the audio version of this book. Simply use the code listed below when visiting our website. Once downloaded to your computer, you can listen to the book through your computer's speakers, burn it to an audio CD or save the file to your portable music device (such as Apple's popular iPod) and listen on the go!

How to get your free audio book digital download:

1. Visit www.tatepublishing.com and click on the e|LIVE logo on the home page.
2. Enter the following coupon code:
   0dc5-daa3-6f3c-5390-b86b-31be-0e3b-ee9f
3. Download the audio book from your e|LIVE digital locker and begin enjoying your new digital entertainment package today!

Made in the USA
Middletown, DE
19 January 2017